CONTINUING EDUCATION FOR FLORIDA REAL ESTATE PROFESSIONALS

FLORIDA

Eleventh Edition

EDWARD J. O'DONNELL

Dearborn
Real Estate Education

This publication is designed to provide accurate and authoritative information in regard to the subject matter covered. It is sold with the understanding that the publisher is not engaged in rendering legal, accounting, or other professional advice. If legal advice or other expert assistance is required, the services of a competent professional should be sought.

President: Dr. Andrew Temte
Chief Learning Officer: Dr. Tim Smaby
Vice President, Real Estate Education: Asha Alsobrooks
Development Editor: Julia Marti

CONTINUING EDUCATION FOR FLORIDA REAL ESTATE PROFESSIONALS
ELEVENTH EDITION
© 2011 by Kaplan, Inc.
Published by DF Institute, Inc., d/b/a Dearborn™ Real Estate Education
332 Front St. S., Suite 501
La Crosse, WI 54601
www.dearbornRE.com

Printed in the United States of America
10   11   12   10   9   8   7   6   5   4   3   2   1
ISBN: 978-1-4277-2613-1 / 1-4277-2613-2
PPN: 1610-3211

Contents

Preface

We have worked hard to make this text as thorough and practical as possible. It contains many features that we hope you like. Icons are placed in the margins to help you identify these features.

 New

New content is clearly marked throughout the book to show you what's changed since your last renewal.

 Forms to Go

A **Forms-To-Go** is in the back of the book, and the symbol to the left will show you when a form is available. The section has FREC registration forms, brokerage relationship disclosures, property management forms such as three-day notices, property condition disclosure forms, and many more. If you think of other forms to include, please let us know.

@ Web.Link

Web links are highlighted throughout the book so you can use the Internet to find more resource material.

IN PRACTICE
The **In Practice** feature helps you apply the law to your own professional practice.

Case studies are important tools for transferring the knowledge gained through reading and lecture into real-world, practical application. Examples of cases prosecuted by the Division of Real Estate are intended to illustrate the enforcement process.

Progress test questions are inserted after important sections of the text to reinforce the material and make the learning process more interactive. The progress tests are for your use. They are not graded by the school and do not affect your course completion. Answers to the progress test questions are found on pages 134 and 135.

A complete review of **every change to Chapter 475, F.S.,** and **every FREC rule change** from January 2008 through August 2010 is included at the end of chapter 1.

In short, we have tried to make keeping up as productive and thorough as possible. The purpose of this material is to show what has changed and to give in-depth coverage to selected parts of the laws. We strongly recommend that you seek competent legal or tax advice before applying any of the information from this book.

ABOUT THE AUTHOR

Edward O'Donnell has been a Florida real estate broker for more than 30 years. He is a former president of the Tallahassee Board of REALTORS® and district vice president of the Florida Association of REALTORS®. Edward is the author of *Post-Licensing Education for Real Estate Sales Associates* and coauthor of the *Florida Real Estate Broker's Guide,* also published by Dearborn™ Real Estate Education.

ACKNOWLEDGMENTS

Many people contributed to the preparation of this edition. Special thanks go to Robert C. Gordon, Bob Hogue School of Real Estate, and Captain Wayne E. Rowlett, Rowlett Real Estate School, for their thoughtful and thorough reviews of the material.

This book would not have been possible without the encouragement and creative ideas shared by the executives and staff at Dearborn™ Real Estate Education. Their confidence and professionalism mixed with good humor made my work enjoyable. Special thanks to Julia Marti and Trude Irons.

Sharon O'Donnell's encouragement and creativity have made it a better book.

Edward J. O'Donnell
August 2010

How to Complete This Continuing Education Course

Thanks for selecting this book to complete your continuing education requirement. We have carefully designed this course to meet the requirements of the Florida Real Estate Commission (FREC), to enhance your professional knowledge and skills, and to be a continuing resource for information on relevant real estate subjects.

WHAT EDUCATION IS REQUIRED BEFORE I RENEW?

Real estate brokers and sales associates must complete 14 hours of continuing education every two years after their first license renewal. This course meets the entire FREC-prescribed continuing education requirements. Chapters 1, 2, and 3 of this book meet the "core law" requirement, and the remaining chapters are selected "specialty education" sections.

WHAT IF THIS IS MY FIRST RENEWAL?

If this is your first renewal after receiving your sales associate or broker license, this course *will not meet the education requirement.* Sales associates who are renewing for the first time must take a 45-hour post-licensing course. Brokers and broker associates who are renewing for the first time must take a 60-hour post-licensing course.

HOW DO I COMPLETE THE CLASSROOM COURSE?

This text has been designed for use in the classroom or to be taken by distance learning. If you are taking this course in the classroom, there is no final examination. If you miss more than 10 percent of the course hours, you will not receive course credit. You may disregard the following information about taking the distance learning course exam if you are taking the classroom course.

HOW DO I COMPLETE THE DISTANCE LEARNING COURSE?

The course does not have to be completed at once. You should take the course at your own pace, at times convenient to you. Complete the progress questions as you go, then check your answers with the key at the back of this book. Continue to the next chapter when it's convenient. Most students will need approximately 14 hours to complete this course. You may complete it in more or less time.

When you have completed all eight chapters, you are ready to take the 30-question final examination. You must answer at least 24 questions (80 percent) correctly to pass. This is an open-book test. You may use the course material and the index as a reference to help you successfully complete the test. Choose the best answer for each question.

HOW DO I GET MY EXAM GRADED?

You should send your answer sheet to the school where you purchased the course. *Do not send it to the publisher!* If you pass, the school will send you a course completion certificate dated the day it grades your answer sheet. If you do not receive a passing grade, you will be notified by the school about how to retake your examination.

This course is also available online. Contact the real estate school that you used to purchase this course to learn how you can complete your education on the Internet next time.

We hope you will select our course when it's time to renew again.

IMPORTANT NOTICE

The course is not completed until you have received your course completion certificate from the school. You should not renew your license until you have received the certificate.

The school that grades your test will not renew your license. You must do that. Do not renew your license until you have a course completion certificate, or you could face disciplinary action by the Florida Real Estate Commission.

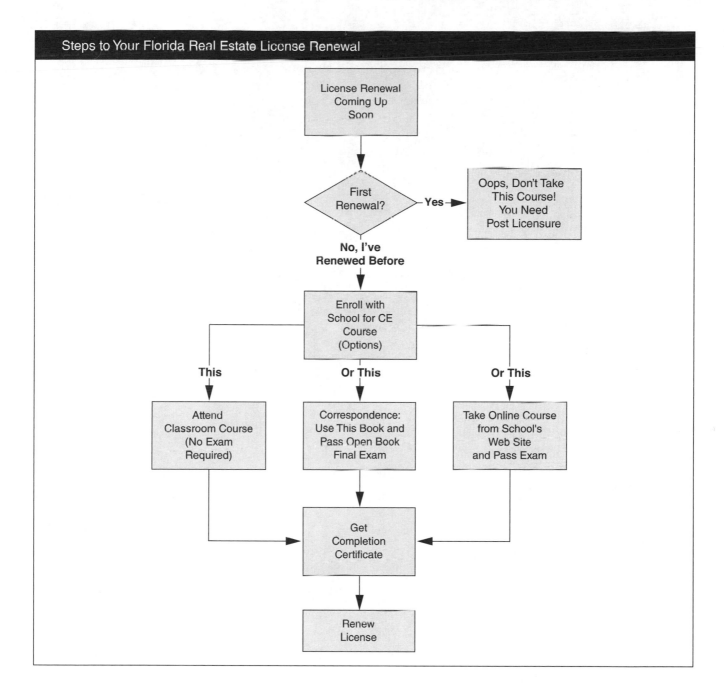

Steps to Your Florida Real Estate License Renewal

Chapter **1**

Real Estate License Law Update

In This Chapter

History of Florida's license law • The Florida Real Estate Commission • Distance learning • Nonresident applicants • License renewal • Inactive licenses • Registration of brokerage entities • Sales associates may be paid directly by the closing agent • Personal assistants • The Florida Landlord and Tenant Act • Brokers who prepare appraisals • Advertising • Changes to Chapter 475, Florida Statutes • Recent changes to FREC rules—Chapter 61J2, Florida Administrative Code

Your Quick Reference Guide to the Major Changes in State Laws

Important changes you should carefully review:

● Broker applicants must have 24 months of experience as a sales associate.

● Sales associates may be licensed as limited liability companies, professional limited liability companies, or professional corporations.

● Prelicense course credits expire if applicant doesn't pass the state exam within two years.

● The Landlord and Tenant Act has changed regarding advance notice that the tenant does not intend to renew the lease.

● Involuntary inactive licensees may have to take a reactivation course.

Learning Objectives

When you have completed this chapter, you should be able to:

● state the criminal charge for unlicensed real estate activity,

● state the number of years a prelicense course is effective when applying for a license,

● list the extra steps required for a nonresident application for licensure,

- describe how to renew a real estate license,
- describe the difference between voluntary and involuntary inactive licenses, and
- describe the activities that may be performed by licensed and unlicensed personal assistants.

HISTORY OF FLORIDA'S LICENSE LAW

The Florida Legislature created Chapter 475, F.S., to regulate the practice of real estate. The law is amended as necessary to continue to protect the public from damage due to fraud or incompetence by licensees. Chapter 475, F.S., has four parts:

- Part I   Real Estate Brokers, Sales Associates, and Schools
- Part II   Appraisers
- Part III   Commercial Real Estate Sales Commission Lien Act
- Part IV   Commercial Real Estate Leasing Commission Lien Act

THE FLORIDA REAL ESTATE COMMISSION

Chapter 475, F.S., created the Florida Real Estate Commission as a consumer protection agency and gave it broad powers to regulate licensees. The Commission has the duty to advance the education of licensees in ethics, law, and brokerage practices. The FREC governs the conduct of licensees, and it has the power to investigate and discipline licensees who violate the law. While the Florida Legislature creates the laws regulating real estate practice in Florida, the Florida Real Estate Commission is charged with making rules that implement the law. The Rules of the Florida Real Estate Commission are Chapter 61J2 of the Florida Administrative Code.

Organization of the Florida Real Estate Commission

The Commission has seven members who are appointed by the governor:

- Four members must be licensed real estate brokers who have had an active license for the previous five years preceding appointments.
- One member may be either a licensed broker or sales associate who has had an active license for at least two years preceding appointment.
- Two members must never have held a real estate license. These members consider real estate issues from a consumer's perspective.
- At least one member must be 60 years old or older. [475.02, F.S.]

Administration of the Real Estate License Law

While the FREC is administratively part of the Department of Business and Professional Regulation (DBPR), the members are not Department employees. The secretary of the DBPR appoints, subject to the approval of the Commission, the director of the Division of Real Estate (DRE). The Division handles the administrative duties involved with carrying out the law.

 Web.Link

Department of Business and Professional Regulation Web site:
www.myfloridalicense.com/dbpr/index.html

A member of the public may:

- search for a license,
- apply for a license,
- view the status of an application, and
- file a complaint.

A licensee may:

- renew a license,
- change license status,
- maintain account,
- change address, and
- view continuing education credits and deficiencies.

The site also has a wide assortment of forms and publications, as well as the statutes and rules affecting real estate.

Forms to Go

While you may change your address or license status using the online service, we have included Forms DBPR 0080-1 (address change) and RE 2050 (change of status) in the Forms-To-Go Section in the back of this book.

PROGRESS QUIZ

1. How many members of the Florida Real Estate Commission must never have held a real estate license?
   a. Seven
   b. Five
   c. Two
   d. One

Real Estate License

Eight activities require that an individual have a real estate license, unless there is a specific exemption in the law. If a person provides one of the eight services for another person for any type of compensation (paid or expected), the person must have an active real estate license. These services are appraise, auction, sell, exchange, buy, rent, lease, or advertise to perform a real estate service. [475.01(1)(a)]

The law includes many exemptions—for example, owners can sell their own properties without having licenses. The law exempts an owner of an apartment complex or a property management firm that pays a finder's fee of not more than $50 to a tenant of the apartment complex. The tenant who receives the fee is also exempt from licensing.

A relatively recent practice by some real estate licensees is the offer to return or "rebate" a portion of the commission to the buyer or the seller in the transaction. Some licensees incorrectly assume this is a violation of Chapter 475. It is not illegal for a licensee to give part of the commission to the buyer or the seller the licensee represents in the transaction, provided that disclosure is made to all interested parties (especially the lender). It must also be shown on the HUD-1 Uniform Settlement Statement if one is used in the transaction.

IN PRACTICE

Be Careful with Rebates and Referral Fees

You can pay a portion of your commission to a buyer or a seller in a transaction; the rebate must be disclosed.

However, you can't pay a fee for referred business (not even a candy bar) to unlicensed persons who are not buyers or sellers. That's illegal!

It is a third-degree felony for an unlicensed person to perform real estate services for others for compensation unless that person is exempt from licensing. [475.42(1)(a)]

Procedure for Becoming Licensed

We know you already have your license, but you may get questions from individuals who want to get in the business. Here are the answers.

An applicant for a real estate sales associate's license must:

- be at least 18 years old,
- have a high school diploma (or equivalent),
- have good character and a reputation for honest dealing, and
- be competent and qualified to perform real estate transactions.

Applicants must submit:

- a complete application,
- fingerprints in an electronic format, and
- the required fee.

An applicant may also apply online through the Department's Web site.

Applicants must disclose whether they have been convicted, pleaded guilty, or pleaded no contest to any crime. If the court withheld adjudication, the conviction must still be disclosed. Florida residents must submit fingerprints electronically. An applicant may have fingerprints scanned at a Pearson VUE testing center in Florida. Pearson VUE will submit the fingerprints to the Florida Department of Law Enforcement and the Federal Bureau of Investigation. Applicants who live outside Florida should send the Division of Real Estate fingerprint card to Pearson VUE's Denver office with a money order for $61. The application will expire two years (formerly one year) after receipt by the Department if the applicant does not pass the state exam.

The applicant must complete the required 63-hour sales associate course (FREC Course I) and achieve a score of at least 70 percent on the end-of-course exam. Applicants for a real estate license who are members of The Florida Bar are exempt from the requirement to take FREC Course I.

Graduates holding a four-year degree in real estate are exempt from sales associate and broker prelicense courses.

Broker Applicants

 New

Before applying for the state exam, a broker applicant must have held an active sales associate license:

- under one or more brokers in any state or foreign jurisdiction for 24 months in the preceding five years (working under an owner-developer does not count unless the employer also holds a broker license); or
- working as a salaried employee of a governmental agency performing the duties authorized for real estate sales associates.

Brokers licensed in another state or jurisdiction for 24 months during the preceding five years also meet the experience requirements to be a Florida broker.

The applicant must complete the broker course with a score of at least 70 percent on the end-of-course exam. The legislature recently repealed a section in Chapter 475 that requires a broker applicant to have been licensed as a sales associate for at least six months before starting the broker course.

Prelicense and post-license students who fail the end-of-course exam may take a different exam within one year without having to retake the entire course, but they must wait at least 30 days after failing the exam. A student who wants to avoid the 30-day wait can retake the entire course before taking a different exam.

Applicants must pass the state exam within two years after passing the education course, or the course becomes invalid for licensure. However, from January 12, 2004, to June 30, 2006, the rule was invalid, meaning that students who completed their courses during that period have no time limit on their course credit. [475.181(2) F.S.]

Broker applicants (except nonresident applicants and university graduates with a four-year degree in real estate) who have been sales associates for fewer than five years must show proof of completion of the sales associate post-license requirement. [475.17, F.S.] [61J2-3.008]

DISTANCE LEARNING

A student has the option of taking a classroom course or a distance learning course (either online or using a CD). Satisfactory completion of a distance learning course requires that the student pass a timed distance learning examination. The FREC cannot require that the final exam be monitored or given at a centralized location.

NONRESIDENT APPLICANTS

An applicant for a Florida real estate license does not have to be a Florida resident, a U.S. citizen, or even a resident of the United States. A nonresident applicant must file an irrevocable consent form, agreeing that lawsuits may be filed against him or her in the Florida county where the plaintiff resides and that legal service in any proceeding may be made to the director of the DRE, with a copy sent to the applicant.

Florida Residency Defined

The FREC defines a Florida resident as:

- a person who has resided in Florida continuously for four calendar months or more within the preceding year, or
- a person who presently resides in Florida with the intention to reside continuously in Florida for four months or more, beginning on the date the person began residency. [61J2-26.002]

It does not matter whether the place of residence is a recreational vehicle, hotel, rental unit, or any other temporary or permanent location. This definition is significant for persons who wish to become Florida licensees under mutual recognition.

A resident licensee who moves out of the state must notify the Commission of the address change within ten days, and comply with all nonresident requirements within 60 days. [475.180, F.S.]

New

Caution!

Mutual recognition is a status available only to nonresidents. A mutual recognition licensee who becomes a Florida resident before making application loses the nonresident benefit and has to take the Florida prelicensing course and the state's 100-point final exam.

Mutual Recognition Agreements

The Commission has *mutual recognition* agreements with nine states: Alabama, Arkansas, Connecticut, Georgia, Indiana, Mississippi, Nebraska, Oklahoma, and Tennessee. Florida's agreements with Colorado and Kentucky expired in 2009. Both states notified Florida that they were offering full reciprocity to sales associates or brokers from any other state who wanted to become licensed in their states, terminating "mutual recognition" agreements. Florida has ongoing negotiations with other states as well. An applicant holding a real estate license in one of these states may become a Florida licensee by passing a 40-question Florida real estate law exam with a score of 75 percent or more. Any Florida licensee can become licensed in one of those states and may contact the appropriate state regulatory agency for an application.

Mutual recognition is not "reciprocity." Reciprocity allows a licensee in one state to work in another state with a reciprocity agreement. Florida does not have reciprocity with any other state. Florida agrees only to mutual recognition of *education* requirements, so licensees cannot qualify for mutual recognition if they obtained their license in the mutual state by reciprocity. The mutual recognition agreements automatically expire every five years unless renewed by the Commission.

PROGRESS QUIZ

3. For how many years is the prelicense course valid?
   a. One
   b. Two
   c. Four
   d. Indefinitely

Nonresident Requirements

Nonresident licensees, whether or not they have qualified under mutual recognition, must successfully complete the same post-licensing and continuing education required for Florida resident licensees.

PROGRESS QUIZ

4. Mary, a veteran Georgia real estate broker, moved to West Palm Beach six months ago. She now wants to get her Florida broker's license. The quickest legal way for her to become a Florida broker is to
   a. first get a Florida sales associate's license, then work for at least one year under one or more Florida brokers, take the required courses, and pass the broker's exam.
   b. pass the 40-question Florida law examination.
   c. take the Florida broker course and pass a 40-question Florida law exam.
   d. pass both the Florida broker course and the state broker's examination.

Computer-Based State Exam

Real estate exams are administered at locations throughout Florida by Pearson VUE, a national testing company. The applicant may request either an English or Spanish exam.

When the DRE approves the applicant for testing, Pearson VUE notifies the applicant by mail. The applicant arranges for a test time, then reports to the exam site with two forms of signature identification, one with a photo; a copy of the course completion slip if the slip was not included with the application; and the confirmation number. Payment must be made in advance; Pearson VUE does not accept payment at the exam site. The exam is taken on a computer provided by the test center.

Forms to Go

The exam is graded immediately, and the applicant is given a pass/fail notice. A passing notice does not show the score, but failure notices show the number of questions answered correctly in each major section of the exam. After passing the exam, the applicant must send a Form RE-2050 signed by the employer to the DBPR by mail or fax to change the license status to active before going to work. If an applicant brings the RE-2050 to the state exam and passes, Pearson VUE's test coordinator will often agree to fax the form to the state immediately.

New licensees may not begin working until the DBPR Web site shows that the license is in active status under the brokerage entity.

IN PRACTICE

The State Exam Is Tough

About 41 to 44 percent of first-time test-takers pass. For applicants who take it more than once, the pass rates are a depressing 26 to 30 percent. Applicants must study, study, study!

LICENSE RENEWAL

Required Education for Renewing an Initial License

Licensees must complete a post-licensing course before the first renewal or their license will be void. The first real estate license is *not* a two-year license. It must be renewed between 18 and 24 months after the license becomes effective because there are only two renewal dates each year: March 31 and September 30

For example, if sales associate Jeannie received her license on April 15, 2008, she must renew by March 31, 2010 (just less than 24 months later). Before renewing, she must successfully complete a 45-hour sales associate post-licensing course or her license will become void. If this happens and Jeannie wants to stay in real estate, she has to start over by taking the prelicensing course and passing the state exam.

Assume that John got his broker license on August 29, 2008. He must complete a 60-hour broker post-licensing course and renew before March 31, 2010, a little more than 19 months later. If he fails to do so, his license becomes void. It's a little different for a broker, however. After John's license becomes void, he may, during the six months following the license becoming void, take a 14-hour continuing education course and apply for sales associate status. If he wishes to become a broker again, he has to successfully complete the broker prelicensing course and pass the state exam. Licensees with a four-year degree in real estate are exempt from sales associate and broker post-licensing requirements. Members of The Florida Bar are not exempt.

Sales associates or brokers who, due to individual physical hardship as defined by rule, cannot complete the courses within the required time may be granted a six-month extension by the Commission. [61J2-3.020]

Required Education for Subsequent Renewals

This course material meets the *entire* 14-hour FREC continuing education requirement.

After the first renewal, a real estate licensee must complete an FREC-approved 14-hour continuing education course before all subsequent renewals. The course consists of three hours of "core law" and 11 hours of "specialty" education. Licensees may take the course in a classroom with no exam or by distance learning with a final exam. Members of The Florida Bar are exempt from the continuing education requirements; licensees with a four-year real estate degree are not exempt.

The core law portion updates licensees on Florida real estate license law, agency law, other state and federal laws, and taxes. FREC gives credit for six hours of core law if the licensee takes the three-hour core law class in each year of the renewal period.

The FREC-approved specialty education course must focus on real estate issues relevant to Chapter 475. Chapters 4 through 8 of this course are the specialty education section. The FREC grants up to three hours of specialty education, one time per renewal cycle, to a licensee who attends an FREC meeting. The licensee must make an appointment with the DRE and stay for the entire day. [475.182(1)(b)]

Continuing education course providers must electronically transmit to the DRE a roster of students who complete the course. The names must be transmitted within 30 days of the course completion. However, the provider must electronically report the completion of a licensee's course within 10 business days beginning on the 30th day before the renewal deadline or prior to the renewal date, whichever occurs sooner.

 **Web.Link**

Procedure for Renewing a License

The department sends a notice of renewal to the last known address of the licensee at least 60 days before the expiration date. Licensees who do not receive a renewal notice should ensure that the department has their current address on file. Failure to receive a renewal notice from the state does not excuse a licensee from completing the education requirement.

Forms to Go

Brokers who change their business address must file a change notice within ten days along with the names of sales associates no longer associated with the firm. This notification also fulfills the change of business address requirements for licensees within the firm. While most brokers do this using the *myfloridalicense.com* Web site, the notice is available in this book and may be mailed or faxed to the DBPR.

Because the firm's license ceases to be in force when a broker moves, the firm may not conduct business until the broker notifies the DRE. The best way to notify the

DRE is by fax, keeping a copy of the receipt, or entering it online. The immediacy of these methods is preferable to the mail because DBPR puts a date/time stamp when the mail is received, not when postmarked.

Sales associates who change their personal mailing address must notify the DRE within ten days by fax, mail, or by using the *myfloridalicense.com* Web site. Violations of this rule may result in a $500 citation. [61J2-24.002]

The normal renewal fee for sales associates is $85 and for brokers is $95. There is a $5 fee that helps the DBPR monitor unlicensed activity. The late fee for renewals is $45.

PROGRESS QUIZ

5. What is the license status of a new sales associate who fails to take the required education and renew a license?
   a. Involuntary inactive
   b. Voluntary inactive
   c. Void
   d. Canceled

DBPR Renewal Procedures

The licensee should not send proof of the required education with the renewal application. The licensee must retain the original grade report for the FREC-approved education course for at least two years following the end of the renewal period.

The DBPR will no longer renew a license if a licensee has not completed the appropriate continuing or post-licensing education. Licensees should obtain the required education in a timely manner to avoid becoming ineligible to work.

 New

Because DBPR will no longer renew a license if the required continuing education course credits or post-licensing course credits have not been recorded in the state database, the penalties for failing to take the required education have been deleted from the FREC rules.

PROGRESS QUIZ

6. For how many years after the end of the renewal date must a licensee retain the course completion grade report for the FREC-prescribed continuing education course?
   a. Four
   b. Three
   c. Two
   d. One

INACTIVE LICENSES

A person must have an active license to perform real estate services for another person for compensation. Many licensees do not work in real estate and have elected to have *voluntary inactive* license status. If these individuals complete the required education and renew every two years, they may remain in this status indefinitely. They may become active at any time without paying a fee by using the *myfloridalicense.com* database, or by mailing or faxing a Form RE-2050.

New

When a license expires and is not renewed, it becomes *involuntary inactive.* After two years, the license will become void. A licensee may reactivate an involuntary inactive license within the first 12 months after expiration by successfully completing the 14-hour continuing education requirement, applying for renewal, and paying the required late renewal fee. If the license has been involuntary inactive for more than 12 months but less than 24 months, the licensee must successfully complete a 28-hour "reactivation" course and pay the required late renewal fees by the end of the second year.

The Florida Real Estate Commission may reinstate the license of an individual whose license has become void if the Commission determines that the individual has made a good-faith effort to renew in compliance with the law but has failed to comply because of illness or unusual hardship. The individual must apply to the Commission for reinstatement in a manner prescribed by rules of the Commission, and shall pay an applicable fee in an amount determined by rule. The individual must meet all continuing education requirements prescribed by law, pay appropriate licensing fees, and otherwise be eligible for renewal of licensure under this chapter.

PROGRESS QUIZ

7. To renew a license that has been involuntary inactive for more than 12 months, but less than 24 months, the licensee must complete
    a. 14 hours of continuing education.
    b. a 28-hour reactivation education course.
    c. 45 hours of post-licensing education.
    d. 63 hours of prelicensing education.

REGISTRATION OF BROKERAGE ENTITIES

Individuals who sell real estate are *licensed*; business entities that employ those licensees must be *registered*. The DBPR registers several types of brokerage organizational structures, including sole proprietorships, general partnerships, limited partnerships, limited liability companies, registered limited liability partnerships, and corporations.

A sales associate or broker associate may register as a professional corporation, limited liability company, or professional limited liability company. A license will be issued in the licensee's legal name only and, when appropriate, shall include the entity designation. The sales associate or broker associate cannot register as a general partner, member, manager, officer, or director of a brokerage firm under Section 475.15. [475.161, F.S.] Sales associates or broker associates (or any other person who is not licensed) can own stock in a brokerage corporation, but no person can own more than 40 percent if they have:

- had a license revoked or suspended that has not been reinstated,
- been convicted of a felony and civil rights have not been restored for at least five years, or
- had an injunction requiring that the individual stop practicing real estate without a license.

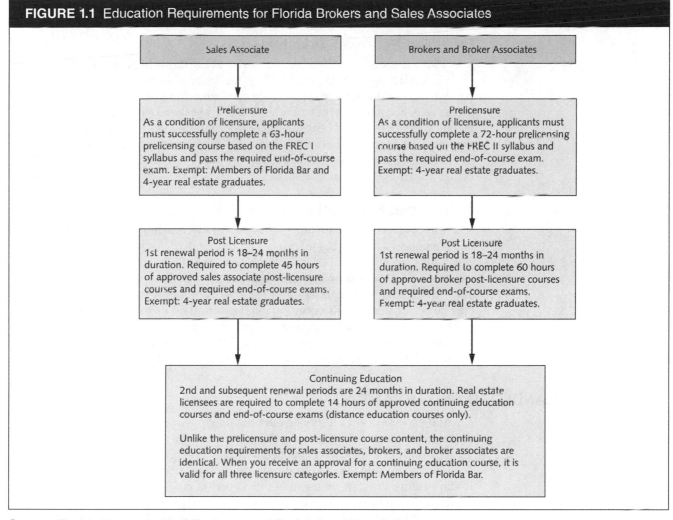

FIGURE 1.1 Education Requirements for Florida Brokers and Sales Associates

Source: Florida Department of Business and Professional Regulation

PROGRESS QUIZ

8. The maximum percentage of a brokerage firm that can be owned by an individual whose real estate license has been revoked is
   a. 0%.
   b. 25%.
   c. 40%.
   d. 100%.

SALES ASSOCIATES MAY BE PAID DIRECTLY BY THE CLOSING AGENT

Brokerage firms may allow sales associates to receive their commissions directly from the closing agent immediately after closing, if the broker gives specific written instructions to the closing agent for each closing. This eliminates the need for a broker to write a check to the sales associate after closing. In no other case may a sales associate collect a commission from a closing agent, buyer, or seller. [FREC Final Order BPR-99-01088]

PERSONAL ASSISTANTS

Licensed Personal Assistants

Many sales associates employ licensed personal assistants because the assistant may provide a full range of real estate services for the customers of the licensees, including showing and listing properties, calling prospects, and providing access to a listed property. A licensed personal assistant must be registered under the employing broker and may be paid for brokerage activities only by the broker. A sales associate may pay the licensed personal assistant for nonselling activities on a salaried or hourly basis, but may not compensate a personal assistant for performance of brokerage activities that require a license.

Unlicensed Personal Assistants

Many licensees employ assistants to help complete routine office activities, such as mass mailings, writing ads, and preparing comparative market analyses. Often these assistants do not have real estate licenses. Licensed sales associates who employ such assistants, as well as their brokers, must ensure that the assistants do not perform any activities that violate the law. In 1992, the FREC approved a list of activities that may be performed by unlicensed personal assistants. The list has not been changed by the FREC since that time, and is shown in Figure 1.2. An unlicensed personal assistant is considered an employee of the licensee. The licensee must withhold and pay payroll taxes as required by the IRS and issue a W-2 form at year-end.

THE FLORIDA LANDLORD AND TENANT ACT

A rental agreement with a specific duration may provide that if a tenant fails to give the required notice before vacating the premises at the end of the rental agreement, the tenant may be liable for liquidated damages as specified in the rental agreement. To collect these damages, the landlord must give written notice to the tenant within 15 days before the start of the notification period contained in the lease describing the tenant's obligations and the date the rental agreement is terminated. The written notice shall list all fees, penalties, and other charges applicable to the tenant. [83.575, F.S.]

BROKERS WHO PREPARE APPRAISALS

A broker or sales associate may prepare a comparative market analysis (CMA) or broker price opinion (BPO) in the normal course of his or her listing and selling activities. It may not be considered an appraisal, and brokers may not call the results of the CMA or BPO an appraisal; it should be called an *opinion of value.* A licensee may charge a fee for preparing a CMA or BPO.

The law does not prohibit licensees from performing appraisals for a fee. Licensees must comply with the *Uniform Standards of Professional Appraisal Practice (USPAP)* when preparing appraisals. The Standards are strict and detailed, and a violation of the Standards is a violation of Chapter 475. Appraisals used in federally related mortgage loans must be prepared by a certified or licensed appraiser. [475.25(1)(t)]

ADVERTISING

The FREC requires that a broker's advertising be done in such a manner that reasonable persons would know they are dealing with a real estate licensee. For example, real estate advertisements, including the print media, business cards, signs, handouts, and novelty items, must include the licensed name of the brokerage firm. If an ad does not include the name of the firm, it is a *blind ad* and violates the law.

FIGURE 1.2 Legal Activities of an Unlicensed Personal Assistant

- Answer the phone and forward calls.
- Fill out and submit listings and changes to any multiple-listing service.
- Follow up on loan commitments after a contract has been negotiated and generally secure status reports on the loan progress.
- Assemble documents for closing.
- Secure documents (public information) from courthouse, utility district, and so on.
- Have keys made for company listings, order surveys, termite inspections, home inspections, and home warranties with the licensed employer's approval.
- Write ads for approval of licensee and supervising broker and place advertising (newspaper ads, update Web sites, etc.); prepare flyers and promotional information for approval by licensee and the supervising broker.
- Receive, record, and deposit earnest money, security deposits, and advance rents.
- Type contract forms for approval by licensee and supervising broker.
- Monitor licenses and personnel files.

- Compute commission checks.
- Place signs on property.
- Order items of repair as directed by the licensee.
- Prepare flyers and promotional information for approval by licensee and supervising broker.
- Act as a courier service to deliver documents and pick up keys.
- Place routine telephone calls on late rent payments.
- Schedule appointments for licensees to show *listed* property.
- Be at an open house:
  1. for security purposes, and/or
  2. to hand out materials (brochures).
- Answer questions concerning a listing from which the answer must be obtained from the licensed employer-approved printed information and is **objective** in nature (not subjective comments).
- Gather information for a comparative market analysis (CMA).
- Gather information for an appraisal.
- Hand out objective, written information on a listing or rental.

Personal Names in an Ad

For a licensee's personal name to appear in a brokerage firm's ad, the licensee's last name as registered with the DRE must be included at least once in the ad. The brokerage firm's name must be included to avoid charges of "blind" advertising. For example, Joseph J. Perkins, a sales associate, could place an advertisement stating "Call Joe for more information," provided the ad includes the brokerage firm's name and Joe's last name, at least once, somewhere in the ad. [61J2-10.025(2)]

Internet Advertising

When advertising on an Internet site, the brokerage firm name must be placed adjacent to or immediately above or below the point of contact information. "Point of contact information" refers to any means for contacting the brokerage firm or individual licensee, including mailing address, physical street address, e-mail address, telephone number, or facsimile telephone number.

IN PRACTICE

Brokers—Check Those Web Pages

Bookmark your sales associates' Web pages in your browser's "favorites" folder and periodically check to ensure they're following the law.

CHANGES TO CHAPTER 475, FLORIDA STATUTES

Stay informed with the summary of changes to Chapter 475, F.S. shown in Figure 1.3.

RECENT CHANGES TO FREC RULES—CHAPTER 61J2, FLORIDA ADMINISTRATIVE CODE

Stay informed on important changes to the law with the summary of Florida Real Estate Commission rule changes between January 2008 and August 2010 (Figure 1.4). This abbreviated summary, sorted by rule number, is for your convenience, but it may not provide a full understanding of the change if the rule is not read in its entirety.

 **Web.Link**   You may obtain a copy of the current Rules of the Florida Real Estate Commission online at: *www.myflorida.com/dbpr/re/statutes.html*

FIGURE 1.3 Florida Statute Changes

Rule	Description of Change
475.17	Requires that applicants for a broker's license have at least 24 months' experience (formerly 12 months) as a: • sales associate under one or more brokers during the preceding five years, • salaried employee of a government agency who has held a sales associate's license for at least 24 months during the preceding five years performing the duties authorized for real estate licensees, or • broker in another state or jurisdiction.
475.451	Removed the requirement that school permit holders or course sponsors send a classroom course roster to the Department.

FIGURE 1.4 Florida Real Estate Commission Rule Changes between January 2008 and August 2010

Rule	Effective Date	Description of Change
61J2-1.011(6)	8-18-08	Removed the text stating that the Commission may conduct seminars and publish and sell documents such as wall certificate of license or course syllabus.
61J2-3.017	4-27-08	Video classroom viewing conditions requirements were repealed. The rule repeal eliminates the obligation of the Commission to regulate viewing conditions for video presentation of courses.
61J2-14.008	6-21-10	Formerly, a broker who deposits customer funds with a title company or attorney had three business days to request written verification of the deposit. The rule was changed to give the broker ten business days. Describes the licensees' obligations when a deposit is placed with an attorney or title company. When escrow funds are placed with a title company or an attorney, the licensee shall indicate on the sales contract the name, address, and telephone number of the title company or attorney. Within ~~three~~ ten business days after each deposit is due under the sales contract, the licensee's broker shall make written request to the title company or attorney to provide written verification of receipt of the deposit. Within ten business days of the date the licensee's broker made the written request for verification of the deposit, the licensee's broker shall provide seller's broker with either a copy of the written verification, or if no verification is received by licensee's broker, written notice that licensee's broker did not receive verification of the deposit. If seller is not represented by a broker, then licensee's broker shall notify the seller directly in the same manner indicated herein.

Case Study

APPLICANT FAILS TO REPORT CRIMINAL HISTORY

● **Facts:** In 2005, the respondent submitted an applicant for a sales associate license. The applicant signed a sworn affidavit that all answers were true, correct, and complete. Question 9 on the application, which asks whether the applicant has ever been convicted of a crime or pleaded nolo contendere, the applicant answered "No." The respondent passed the sales associate examination and was issued a license. The DBPR later received the results of state and federal records search, which revealed a criminal history not disclosed on the application.

1. In 1991, the respondent was adjudicated guilty of robbery with a weapon, a first-degree felony, and sentenced to three and a half years in prison. The Department of Business and Professional Regulation filed an administrative complaint against the licensee.

2. Respondent maintained that, based on a telephone conversation with someone at the Brevard County Courthouse and the fact that she is a notary, registered voter, served on a jury, and is a licensed minister, the record of her criminal activity had been expunged.

3. The administrative law judge determined that the respondent did not initiate any action to cause her criminal record to have been expunged or sealed by court order, nor did she make any reasonably prudent inquiry regarding the status of her criminal record before answering Question 9 on the application.

● **Questions**

1. Did the respondent obtain her license by fraud, misrepresentation, or concealment, thus violating Subsection 475.25(1) (m)?

2. Do you agree with the applicant that she should be allowed to keep her license?

3. What penalty should be assessed against the sales associate?

● **Determination of Violation:** The administrative law judge (ALJ) rejected the sales associate's arguments. The ALJ found the applicant had violated the law and recommended that the respondent's license be revoked and that she be charged fees in accordance with Subsection 455.227(3), Florida Statutes.

● **Penalty:** The Florida Real Estate Commission ordered that the respondent's license be revoked.

Chapter 2

Escrow Accounts and Disciplinary Action

In This Chapter

Escrow accounts ● Property management escrow deposits ● Advance fees ● Retention of records ● Violations and penalties ● Real Estate Recovery Fund

Important changes you should carefully review:

● Requirements for advance fees have been abolished.

● Brokers will be given a reasonable time to correct escrow account errors.

● The maximum fine the FREC may impose has been increased to $5,000 (formerly $1,000) for each separate offense.

● Violations of Chapter 475 have a five-year statute of limitations.

● The Commission must promptly report any criminal violation related to the practice of real estate to the proper prosecuting authority.

● The Recovery Fund will pay fees and court attorneys' costs to brokers who defend against a suit filed as a result of an EDO.

Learning Objectives

When you have completed this chapter, you should be able to:

● differentiate between the amount of personal funds that a broker may place into a sales escrow account versus a property management escrow account,

● calculate the last dates for depositing funds received from a customer,

● describe the exemptions that allow a broker to disburse escrowed funds without securing the written approval of both seller and buyer,

● list the four settlement procedures for escrow disputes,

● list the information that is required to be on the broker's entrance sign,

- list the steps required to file a claim for payment from the Real Estate Recovery Fund,
- list the maximum amounts the Florida Real Estate Commission (FREC) will disburse from the Recovery Fund, and
- list the DRE's three responses to license law violations.

ESCROW ACCOUNTS

Buyers customarily give a deposit to a broker to accompany their offer for a property. While such a deposit is not required to form a contract, it shows their "good-faith" intent to close the transaction as promised. The deposit is called a *good-faith deposit* or an *earnest money deposit*. Some brokers call it a *binder deposit*.

The FREC vigorously enforces the escrow laws to ensure that consumers may safely entrust their money to a broker. The rigid enforcement guidelines are in the best interests of the real estate industry.

Maintaining an Escrow Account

An *escrow account* means an account in a bank, trust company, title company having trust powers, credit union, or a savings association within the state of Florida. These accounts hold funds that belong to persons other than the broker. At least one broker in the firm must be authorized to sign checks on the escrow account. Other members of the firm may also be authorized to sign checks. [61J2-14.008(1)(c)] [61J2-14.010(1)]

A broker may deposit up to $1,000 of personal or business funds to open a sales escrow account, or $5,000 to open a property management escrow account, keep it open, and pay for account service charges. [61J2-14.010(2)]

IN PRACTICE

You Don't Need a Trust Account

Let a title company hold the deposits. You save time accounting and record keeping, never have to worry about conflicting demands for deposits, and eliminate the need for DBPR escrow audits.

Timely Deposit of Funds Received

A sales associate who receives any deposit must deliver it to the broker no later than the business day following receipt. Brokers who maintain an escrow account must deposit the funds no later than the end of the third business day following receipt of the funds from the customer (not from date of receipt from the sales associate). The time period is not cumulative. A broker is not responsible if the bank dishonors a check unless the broker, by culpable negligence, failed to deposit the check on time and a party is damaged as a result. [61J2-14.008(1)(b)] Saturdays, Sundays, and legal holidays are not counted as business days. [61J2-14.009]

Example: John Sousa signed a purchase agreement and gave sales associate Wendell an earnest money deposit on Thursday afternoon for $5,000. Wendell must deliver the deposit to his broker, Larry, by the end of the next business day, Friday. Broker Larry must deposit the funds no later than the end of business on Tuesday.

 Forms to Go

A sample Notice of Dishonored Check is in the Forms-To-Go section.

Interest-Bearing Escrow Accounts

A broker who has the written permission of all parties to a transaction may place funds in an interest-bearing escrow account. The permission document must set the time to disburse earned interest and name the person to receive the interest. The escrow account must be insured and held in a depository within the state of Florida. [61J2-14.014]

When the Deposit Is Held by a Title Company or Attorney

 New

When a deposit is placed with a title company or an attorney, the licensee who prepared or presented the sales contract must indicate on that contract the name, address, and telephone number of such title company or attorney. Within ten (formerly three) business days after each deposit is due under the sales contract, the licensee's broker must make written request to the title company or attorney to provide written verification of receipt of the deposit.

Within ten business days of the date the licensee's broker made the written request for verification of the deposit, the licensee's broker must provide the seller's broker with either a copy of the written verification or, if no verification is received by licensee's broker, written notice that licensee's broker did not receive verification of the deposit. If the seller is not represented by a broker, then licensee's broker shall notify the seller directly.

When the deposit is held by a title closing agent or attorney, the following sections about conflicting demands do not apply. Closing agents and attorneys normally will not release any funds unless they have (1) the written agreement of both parties or (2) a court order.

Disbursing Funds from a Broker's Escrow Account

> The broker is custodian of escrow funds. Legal control rests with other parties.

The broker is the custodian of escrowed funds but does not legally control the funds. The buyer has legal control of escrowed funds and may demand return of the funds at any time until the seller has accepted a buyer's offer. Upon acceptance, however, both the buyer and the seller legally control the deposit. The broker should not disburse the funds without the written agreement of both the buyer and the seller. [61J2-14.011]

Conflicting Demands for Escrowed Funds

When both seller and buyer demand the release of escrowed funds without agreeing who will receive the funds, it is known as *conflicting demands.* If no demand has been made for the escrowed funds, but the broker is uncertain about who is entitled to the funds, the broker is said to have *good-faith doubt.*

For example, if a contract clause states that the buyer may void the contract if termite damage exceeds $1,000, and a contractor's estimate to repair the damage is $1,500, there may be good-faith doubt. If the broker tries to contact the seller repeatedly, and the seller does not respond, the broker may then decide to disburse the escrowed funds to the buyer, arguing that he did not have a good-faith doubt as to the buyer being entitled to the funds. While the broker may be safe from disciplinary action from the FREC, the seller may still sue him and might win the case.

Procedures in Escrow Deposit Disputes

The broker holding the escrow deposit has 15 business days to send written notification to the FREC after receiving the last conflicting demand from the buyer or seller or after having good-faith doubt. A Notice of Escrow Dispute form is in the Forms-To-Go section. Within 30 business days after the last demand, the broker must begin one of the following settlement procedures:

- Request the Commission to issue an escrow disbursement order determining who is entitled to the escrowed property. This may be done by using the Request for Escrow Disbursement Order form included in the Forms-To-Go section.
- Submit the dispute for mediation, if all parties agree. Payment to the mediator must be agreed to in writing. Mediation does not produce a binding decision, but it is a method to help the parties reach an agreement. If the parties have not reached agreement within 90 days, the broker must promptly select one of the other measures.
- Submit the dispute for arbitration, provided all parties agree. Under arbitration, the parties agree to be legally bound by the decision and to pay the arbitrator.
- Submit the dispute to litigation by a court, either by interpleader or declaratory decree. If a broker claims no part of the deposit, the court action would be called an *interpleader*. If the broker were claiming part of the escrow deposit, the broker would ask the court for a declaratory judgment. [475.25(1)(d)1]

PROGRESS QUIZ

11. Which of the conflicting demands settlement procedures is employed if a broker wants the court system to handle the dispute?
    a. Arbitration
    b. Litigation
    c. Mediation
    d. Escrow disbursement order

Exceptions to the Conflicting Demands Requirements

Brokers who disburse disputed escrowed funds held on a contract without following the conflicting demands procedures may be charged with *failing to account and deliver escrowed property*. There are currently three exceptions. A broker may return the escrowed property without notifying the Commission if:

- the buyer of a residential condominium unit delivers to the licensee written notice of the buyer's intent to cancel the contract during the statutory "cooling off" period, or
- the buyer of real property in good faith fails to satisfy the terms in the financing clause of the contract, or
- the funds concern a HUD contract for HUD-owned property, in which case the broker must follow HUD's Agreement to Abide, Broker Participation Requirements.

Chapter 475 requires the FREC to adopt rules describing additional exceptions.

> **IN PRACTICE**
>
> **Be Careful Using the Financing Clause Contingency Exception**
> If you decide to give the deposit back to a buyer who failed to get the financing, be careful. These exceptions protect you from administrative action by the FREC, but if you are sued and the seller proves the buyer didn't use best efforts to get the loan, you could lose a court case. If in doubt, always get a signed release from both parties before disbursing the funds.

Brokers' Rights to Deposits for Commissions

If the party entitled to escrowed funds disputes the broker's commission claim, the broker may retain the amount of the claim in the escrow account until the dispute is settled by agreement, arbitration, mediation, or a court order. [61J2-14.011]

PROPERTY MANAGEMENT ESCROW DEPOSITS

Brokers who manage property must make timely deposits, just as brokers who deal in listings and sales. While there is no legal requirement that a broker maintain separate accounts for rental and sales deposits, the Commission recommends separate accounts for sales, rents, advance rents, and security deposits for rental properties. This practice makes accounting and auditing easier.

Disposition of Security Deposits

The broker must either return the security deposit within 15 days after the end of the lease or give written notice to the tenant within 30 days (formerly 15 days) of intent to impose a claim on the deposit. The notice must be sent by certified mail to the tenant's last known mailing address and include the reason for imposing the claim. [Chapter 83.49(3)(a)] A Notice of Claim on Security Deposit is in the Forms-To-Go section.

 Forms to Go

Conflicting Demands Between Landlord and Tenant

If the tenant fails to respond, the broker may disburse the funds to the landlord. A tenant who objects must notify the broker in writing within 15 days from the time the tenant receives the broker's notice. When a tenant disputes the notice to impose a claim on the security deposit and the broker has followed the requirements of Chapter 83 by sending the notice within 30 days, there is no requirement that the FREC be notified of the conflicting demands. The broker may disburse the deposit as the broker sees fit; however, the exemption from having to notify the FREC will not protect the broker from a lawsuit by the tenant or the property owner to recover the funds.

The language in the Florida Landlord and Tenant Act is as follows:

> Compliance with this section by an individual or business entity authorized to conduct business in this state, *including Florida-licensed real estate brokers and sales associates*, shall constitute compliance with all other relevant Florida statutes pertaining to security deposits held pursuant to a rental agreement or other landlord-tenant relationship. Enforcement personnel shall look solely to this section to determine compliance. This section *prevails over any conflicting provisions in Chapter 475* and in other sections of the Florida Statutes, and shall operate to permit licensed real estate brokers to disburse security deposits and deposit money without having to comply with the notice and settlement procedures contained in 475.25(1)(d), F.S. [Chapter 83.49(3)(d)]

Disbursement to Property Owners

Brokers who manage property are under pressure from owners who want their checks as soon as possible after the first of the month collections. Brokers must be wary of disbursing funds from the property management escrow account before the rent checks clear the tenant's bank. If a tenant's check were dishonored, the broker would be using other people's escrow money, a serious violation.

IN PRACTICE

Protect Yourself from Bounced Tenant Checks

If you manage a lot of properties, you're at risk for bounced checks. Put the maximum $5,000 in the property management escrow account to protect against dishonored checks. Wait until you are satisfied that the tenant's check has cleared. If a tenant bounces several personal checks, consider requiring cashier's checks or money orders.

Brokers' Records

Brokers must maintain accurate records of escrow account transactions. Upon request, the broker must make those records available to the Department of Business and Professional Regulation (DBPR) or its investigator, including deposit receipts, bank statements, and all agreements between the parties to a transaction. [61J2-14.012(1)]

Forms to Go

The broker must have a reconciliation prepared at least monthly, comparing the broker's total trust liability with the reconciled bank balances of all escrow accounts. The broker must date and sign each reconciliation. A reconciliation form is included in the Forms-To-Go section. Provided that there is not a shortage in the account, that there is no danger to the public, and it's a first offense, brokers will be given a notice of noncompliance giving reasonable time to correct escrow account errors.

The minimum information required in the monthly reconciliation includes the following:

- Reconciliation date
- Bank name
- Bank account name
- Bank account number
- Account balance
- Dates and numbers of outstanding checks
- An itemized list of the broker's trust liability (names of parties and the amounts owed to each)

- Other items necessary to reconcile the account
- Broker's checkbook balance
- Other records showing the date of receipt and source of the funds [61J2-14.012(2)]

If the trust (escrow) liability and the bank balances do not agree, the reconciliation must explain the difference. The broker must describe the corrective action taken if there is any shortage or overage in the account.

ADVANCE FEES

In 2006, the Florida Legislature abolished regulation of advance fees by repealing Section 475.452 of the Florida Statutes. It is not illegal for brokers to hold advance fees as long as the broker uses responsible trust account practices It is, however, still illegal for any real estate broker, broker associate, or sales associate to collect an advance fee for the listing of a time-share estate or time-share license. [721.20(6)]

RETENTION OF RECORDS

A broker must retain all escrow account records for at least five years from the date of receipt of any funds. The five-year requirement also applies to any listing agreement, purchase offer, property management agreement, or lease agreement. A broker must retain brokerage relationship disclosures in all transactions that result in a written contract to purchase and sell real property for five years or at least two years after the conclusion of litigation, whichever is later. [475.5015, F.S.]

VIOLATIONS AND PENALTIES

Procedure for Filing a Complaint

A consumer may file a complaint against a licensee by sending a Uniform Complaint Form to the Division of Real Estate (DRE) by mail or fax. Complaints may also be filed online. The complaint must identify the licensee and state the allegations. Copies of relevant documents (e.g., contracts and checks) should be included with the complaint.

 Web.Link

Go to *www.myfloridalicense.com/entercomplaint.asp?SID=*

When the Division receives a complaint, a complaint analyst decides if the complaint is "legally sufficient." A complaint is considered legally sufficient if it alleges a violation of a Florida statute, a DBPR rule, or a FREC rule. When violations are supported by documentation, a case number is assigned and the case is forwarded to the investigative field office closest to the location of the licensee who is the subject of the complaint. Unless the nature of the complaint requires a confidential investigation, the subject of the complaint will be given a copy of the complaint by the DRE and requested to respond to the allegations. A complaint analyst with the Division will respond to the complainant within three weeks.

A complaint without sufficient information to support the claimed violation is assigned a case number, and the complainant is informed that no case will be opened. The complaint is retained as part of the Division's records.

A complaint does not become public information until ten days after probable cause has been found or until ten days after the subject of the investigation waives the privilege of confidentiality. [455.25(4), F.S.] If probable cause is found, the DBPR will file a formal complaint against the licensee. The license of a licensee who fails to answer the formal complaint within 20 days will usually be revoked.

The licensee has three options:

- Request a formal hearing in order to dispute the charges. In this case, an administrative law judge will hear the evidence in the hearing and prepare a recommended order showing the judge's findings and recommending the penalty to be applied. The recommended order is forwarded to the DRE and the other parties in the case.
- Request an informal hearing before the Florida Real Estate Commission members who were not members of the Probable Cause Panel for the case. The licensee must admit to the charges, and then a final order is drafted describing the penalties to be applied.
- Agree to a stipulation, which is a voluntary agreement between the licensee and the DRE.

The FREC can fine, suspend, revoke, order probation, or reprimand real estate licensees, but it has no authority to order restitution or payment of money. In 2006, the law was changed to allow the FREC to impose an administrative fine not to exceed $5,000 for each separate offense. The maximum fine was formerly $1,000 for each offense.

An administrative complaint against a licensee must be filed within five years after the time of the act giving rise to the complaint, or within five years after the time the act is discovered or should have been discovered with the exercise of due diligence. [475.25(5), F.S.]

The Commission must promptly report to the proper prosecuting authority any criminal violation of any statute relating to the practice of real estate regulated by the Commission. [475.25(6), F.S.] The Department must promptly notify a licensee's broker or employer when a formal complaint is filed against the licensee alleging violations of this chapter or Chapter 455. The Department shall not issue a notification to the broker or employer until ten days after a finding of probable cause has been found to exist by the Probable Cause Panel or by the Department or until the licensee waives the privilege of confidentiality under Section 455.225, whichever occurs first.

IN PRACTICE

Administrative Complaint? Get an Attorney

Brokers and sales associates who are notified that the FREC has filed an administrative complaint against them should immediately hire a lawyer with experience in administrative law. Even attorneys don't try to represent themselves in a case; you shouldn't either.

Brokerage Office Inspections and Audits

The DRE conducts a routine inspection of every brokerage office at least once every five years to ensure compliance with the real estate license law. The Division investigator ordinarily sends the broker a letter first, then phones to arrange a time to visit the office for an audit. The investigator checks for compliance in the following areas:

- **Office requirements.** There must be at least one enclosed room in a stationary building.
- **Office entrance sign.** The sign must be easily observed and read by anyone entering the office. The sign must have the name of the broker, a partnership or corporate name or trade name, if any, and the words "Licensed (or "Lic.") Real Estate Broker."

- **Brokerage relationship disclosures.** Brokers must retain required disclosures on contracts for sale and purchase of residential properties for at least five years. (These disclosures are discussed in chapter 4.)
- **Licenses.** Licenses and registration of the firm and all its members are verified to ensure that all persons involved in providing real estate services have current licenses.
- **Escrow accounts.** The investigator reviews monthly reconciliation statements for several months as well as bank deposit receipts, pending sales contracts, and property management contracts.

IN PRACTICE

When Notified That a DBPR Inspector Will Be Visiting, Check *Everything*

Make certain to check that your sign is in compliance, all required disclosures are in the transaction folders, reconciliations are dated and signed, and all sales associate licenses are in order.

REAL ESTATE RECOVERY FUND

The Real Estate Recovery Fund was established to compensate individuals or entities that lose money due to an offense by a real estate broker or sales associate in a real estate transaction. The fund is replenished by:

- fees paid by licensees at renewal,
- fines imposed by the Commission and collected by the Department, and
- repayments to the fund by licensees who have judgments against them.

If the fund at any time exceeds $1 million, collections of licensees' fees stop and will not start again unless the fund balance drops below $500,000.

Procedure for Filing a Claim

To be paid from the fund, the consumer must:

> The consumer must have an uncollectible judgment against an active licensee for wrongdoing.

- have received a final judgment from a Florida civil court against an individual broker or sales associate (not a corporation or partnership) in any action based on a real estate brokerage transaction. The Commission may waive the need for a final judgment due to the death or bankruptcy of the licensee;
- make the claim for recovery within two years of the act or within two years from the time the act was discovered but in no event later than four years after the act occurred;
- cause a writ of execution to be issued on the judgment and sign an affidavit that no personal or real property of the debtor can be found or levied upon;
- file a claim with the FREC or the Department of Legal Affairs by certified mail; and
- execute an affidavit showing that the final judgment in the case is not on appeal or, if it were the subject of an appeal, that the appellate process has concluded and the appeal upheld the judgment.

Amount to Be Reimbursed

The fund will reimburse compensatory damages, but not punitive damages, up to $50,000 for judgments in one transaction against a licensee, regardless of the number of claimants. If there are several judgments for more than one transaction, the maximum amount that will be paid from the fund for one licensee is $150,000. The fund will not pay treble damages, court costs, attorneys' fees, or interest.

Penalties for Payments from the Fund

Upon payment from the fund in settlement of a claim against a licensee, the license of the broker or sales associate is automatically suspended the same day. A hearing is not necessary. The license shall not be reinstated until the licensee has repaid in full, plus interest, the amount paid from the fund.

Disbursements for Broker's Compliance with an Escrow Disbursement Order

One exception to the penalty just described involves payment from the fund when a broker suffers a financial loss resulting from following an escrow disbursement order (EDO). The Commission will reimburse the broker for the amount of the loss and take no disciplinary action against the broker. Under the most recent law change, the FREC will also pay the broker's reasonable attorney's fees and court costs. If the plaintiff prevails in court, the Commission will pay the plaintiff's reasonable attorney's fees and court costs. [475.482, F.S.] [475.483, F.S.] [475.484, F.S.]

DRE's Three Responses to License Law Violations

The DRE has three levels of response to violations: notification of noncompliance, citation, and administrative complaint.

Notification of noncompliance. For a first-time minor offense, the DRE may issue a notification of noncompliance. The Division must identify the statute or rule violated (see Figure 2.1), show how the violation can be corrected, and allow 15 days for compliance. A minor violation is defined by the FREC as one that does not endanger the health, safety, or welfare of the public. This should be considered a warning, and the licensee who receives the notice should take corrective action within the required time limit or face more serious penalties. [61J2-24.003]

Citation. In some situations, DRE investigators have the authority to issue a citation. (See Figure 2.2.) It usually involves an offense that is not a substantial threat to the public, such as failing to maintain the required office entrance sign. The principal purpose of the citation rule is to reduce the time and expense of other disciplinary actions. Citations are served on the subject either by personal service or certified mail (restricted delivery) to the subject's last known address.

Citations usually require that a licensee either pay a fine from $100 to $1,000 within 30 days or dispute the charge in writing and begin the formal hearing process. All fines are payable to the "Department of Business and Professional Regulation—R.E. Citations" and are sent to the Division of Real Estate. A copy of the citation should accompany the payment. If not disputed within 30 days, the citation becomes a final order of the Commission. [61J2-24.002]

Administrative complaint. The FREC has established a range of disciplinary guidelines from which penalties will be imposed on licensees guilty of violating Chapters 455 or 475, F.S. (See Figure 2.3.) The maximum fine for an administrative complaint (formerly $1,000) has been increased to $5,000. The purpose of the guidelines is to give notice to the licensees of the range of penalties that will normally be imposed for each count during a formal or informal hearing. [61J2-24.001]

No penalty brought against the broker for EDO-related disbursements.

Did You Know . . .

The most common violations resulting in administrative complaints in 2008 were violation of statutes or FREC or DBPR rules; fraud or deceit in real estate practice; and practicing without a license, registration, or certification.

 New

PROGRESS QUIZ

13. The maximum fine for violating Chapter 475, F.S. is
    a. $5,000.
    b. $3,000.
    c. $1,000.
    d. any amount determined to be reasonable by the FREC final order panel.

FIGURE 2.1 Notification of Noncompliance Guidelines [61J2-24.003] as of June 1, 2010

(a)	61J2-3.009(5)(e)	Failure to have a distance education instructor available
(b)	61J2-3.009(6)	Failure to inform students of course standards and requirements
(c)	61J2-3.015(2)	Failure to provide a course completion report to a student
(d)	61J2-5.016	Sales associate or broker–sales associate serving as an officer or director of a registered brokerage corporation
(e)	61J2-10.024	Failure to maintain the office entrance sign as required
(f)	61J2-10.032(1)	Failure to perform the required act within the stated time frame but does so no later than 30 days after the stated time frame
(g)	61J2-10.034	Failure to register a trade name with the Division of Real Estate
(h)	61J2-14.008(2)(b) **New**	Initial offense of failure to indicate the name, address and telephone number of the title company or attorney on the contract will receive a notice of non-compliance without citation for a period of twelve months after the effective date of this rule.
(i)	61J2-14.008(2)(b) **New**	Initial offense of failure to provide Seller's broker, or Seller if not presented by a broker, within ten (10) business days of the date the Licensee's broker made the written request for verification of the deposit with either a copy of the written verification, or if no verification is received by Licensee's broker, written notice that Licensee's broker did not receive verification of the deposit, will receive a notice of non-compliance without citation for a period of twelve months after the effective date of this rule.
(j)	61J2-14.012	Failure to sign the escrow account reconciliation if the account balances
(k)	61J2-14.014(2)	Failure to stop interest from accruing prior to disbursement
(l)	475.451(8) **New**	Failure to keep registration records, course, rosters, attendance records, a file copy of each examination and progress test, and all student answer sheets for a period of at least 3 years subsequent to the beginning of each course and make them available to the department for inspection and copying upon request.
(m)	61J2-17.014	Improper use of a guest lecturer
(n)	61J2-17.015	Improper recruiting; failure to post the required statement

FIGURE 2.2	Citation Guidelines as of June 1, 2010	
(a)	475.180(2)(a)–A nonresident failed to file the required irrevocable consent form; a resident licensee who failed to notify the Commission of becoming a nonresident as prescribed	$300
(b)	475.17(2)(a), 475.17(3)(a), 475.17(4)(a), 61J2-3.008, and 61J2-3.009–Failed to provide the required number of classroom hours for an approved or prescribed course	$500
(c)	475.175(2) and 61J2-17.012(2)–Failed to provide a course roster to the Division for each course	$100
(d)	475.175(2) and 61J2-3.015–Failed to provide a course completion report to a student	$100
(e)	475.22(1) and 61J2-10.022–Failed to maintain the required office as prescribed	$500
(f)	475.22(1) and 61J2-10.024–Failed to maintain the required office entrance sign	$100
(g)	475.22(2)–Failed to register an out-of-state Florida broker's office	$500
(h)	475.24, 61J2-8.003, and 61J2-10.023–Failed to register a location as a branch office	$200
(i)	475.25(1)(k) and 61J2-14.008(1)(d)–Failed to immediately deposit trust funds, provided the deposit is not more than three days late	$200
(j)	475.25(1)(q)–Failed to give the appropriate disclosure or notice at the appropriate time under the provisions of Sections 475.2755 or 475.278. (A citation may be given only for a first-time violation.)	$300
(k)	475.25(1)(r)–Failed to include the required information in a listing agreement; failed to give a copy to a principal within 24 hours; contains a self-renewal clause	$200
(l)	475.42(1)(b)–Sales associate operating as a sales associate without a registered employer due to failure to renew or properly register	$500
(m)	475.42(1)(j)–Having a lis pendens placed by an attorney. (Citation may be issued only if no other violation is present.)	$500
(n)	475.42(1)(k) and 61J2-10.034–Operated as a broker under a trade name without causing the trade name to be noted in the records of the Commission	$500
(o)	475.451(3)–Failed to obtain a multiple permit	$500
(p)	475.4511(2)–Advertised false, inaccurate, misleading, or exaggerated information	$500

FIGURE 2.2 Citation Guidelines as of June 1, 2010 (continued)

(q)	61J2-3.009(4)(d)–Failed to have a distance education course instructor available per published schedule	$300	**New**
(r)	61J2-3.009(5)(a)–Failed to inform students of course standards and requirements	$100	**New**
(s)	61J2-3.015(2)–Failed to provide a course completion report to a student; if a licensee, as the result of an audit/inspection, failed to provide a course completion report to the DBPR	$200	
(t)	61J2-5.016–Sales associate or broker associate serving as an officer or director of a registered brokerage corporation	$200	
(u)	61J2-5.019(1)–Failed to ensure that the corporation or partnership is properly registered; failed to ensure that each officer, director, and sales associate is properly licensed	$500	
(v)	61J2-10.025–Advertised in a manner in which a reasonable person would not know one is dealing with a real estate licensee or brokerage; failed to include the registered name of the brokerage firm in the advertisement; failed to use the licensee's last name, as registered with the Commission, in an advertisement	$500	
(w)	61J2-10.027–Used the name or identification of an association or organization when the licensee was not in good standing or otherwise not entitled to use same	$300	
(x)	61J2-10.032(1)–Broker failed to notify the Commission within the prescribed 15 business days but does so within 25 business days; or, if a Notice of Noncompliance has been issued pursuant to 61J2-24.003 and not timely complied with, failed to notify the Commission within 45 days but does so within 55 days	$100	
(y)	61J2-10.032(1) and (2)–Broker failed to institute a settlement procedure within the prescribed 30 business days but does so within 40 business days; or, if a Notice of Noncompliance has been issued pursuant to 61J2-24.003 and not timely complied with, failed to institute a settlement procedure within 60 days but does so within 70 days	$100	
(z)	61J2-10.032(2)–Broker failed to notify the Commission that the dispute settled or went to court, or of the final accounting and disbursement within the prescribed 10 business days but broker does so within 20 business days; or, if a Notice of Noncompliance has been issued pursuant to 61J2-24.003 and not timely complied with, failed to notify the Commission that the dispute settled or went to court, or of the final accounting and disbursement within 40 days but does so within 50 days	$100	

FIGURE 2.2 Citation Guidelines as of June 1, 2010 (continued)

(aa)	61J2-10.038–Failed to timely notify the DBPR of the current mailing address or any change in the current mailing address	$500
(bb)	61J2-14.008(2)(b)–Second offense failure to indicate the name, address and telephone number of the title company or attorney on the contract	$200　**New**
(cc)	61J2-14.008(2)(b)–Second offense failure to provide Seller's broker, or Seller if not presented by a broker, within ten (10) business days of the date the Licensee's broker made the written request for verification of the deposit with either a copy of the written verification, or if no verification is received by Licensee's broker, written notice that Licensee's broker did not receive verification of the deposit	$500　**New**
(dd)	61J2-14.012(2)–Failed to properly reconcile an escrow account when the account balances	$500
(ee)	61J2-14.014(1)–Failed to secure the written permission of all interested parties prior to placing trust funds in an interest-bearing escrow account	$300
(ff)	61J2-14.014(2)–Failed to stop interest from accruing prior to disbursement	$100
(gg)	61J2-17.013(1)–Guaranteed that a pupil would pass an examination	$500
(hh)	Failed to register a school location	$500
(ii)	61J2-17.014–Improper use of a guest lecturer	$100
(jj)	61J2-17.015–Failed to post the required language regarding recruitment for employment; recruiting for employment opportunities during class time	$300

FIGURE 2.3 FREC Disciplinary Guidelines as of August 31, 2010

(1)   Pursuant to Section 455.2273, F.S., the Commission sets forth below a range of disciplinary guidelines from which disciplinary penalties will be imposed upon licensees guilty of violating Chapter 455 or 475, F.S. The purpose of the disciplinary guidelines is to give notice to licensees of the range of penalties which normally will be imposed for each count during a formal or an informal hearing. For purposes of this rule, the order of penalties, ranging from lowest to highest, is: reprimand, fine, probation, suspension, and revocation or denial. Pursuant to Section 475.25(1), F.S., combinations of these penalties are permissible by law. Nothing in this rule shall preclude any discipline imposed upon a licensee pursuant to a stipulation or settlement agreement, nor shall the range of penalties set forth in this rule preclude the Probable Cause Panel from issuing a letter of guidance.

(2)   As provided in Section 475.25(1), F.S., the Commission may, in addition to other disciplinary penalties, place a licensee on probation. The placement of the licensee on probation shall be for such a period of time and subject to such conditions as the Commission may specify. Standard probationary conditions may include, but are not limited to, requiring the licensee: to attend pre-licensure courses; to satisfactorily complete a pre-licensure course; to attend post-licensure courses; to satisfactorily complete a post-licensure course; to attend continuing education courses; to submit to and successfully complete the state-administered examination; to be subject to periodic inspections and interviews by a DBPR investigator; if a broker, to place the license on a broker associate status; or, if a broker, to file escrow account status reports with the Commission or with a DBPR investigator at such intervals as may be prescribed.

(3)   The penalties are as listed unless aggravating or mitigating circumstances apply pursuant to subsection (4). The verbal identification of offenses is descriptive only; the full language of each statutory provision cited must be consulted in order to determine the conduct included.

| Violation | | Penalty Range | | |
		First Violation		Second and Subsequent Violations
(a)	Section 475.22, F.S. Broker fails to maintain office or sign at entrance of office	(a)	Reprimand to $500 administrative fine	(a) 90-day suspension and $1,000 administrative fine
(b)	Section 475.24, F.S. Failure to register a branch office	(b)	Reprimand to $500 administrative fine	(b) 90-day suspension and $1,000 administrative fine
(c)	Section 475.25(1)(b), F.S. Fraud, misrepresentation, and dishonest dealing Concealment, false promises, false pretenses by trick, scheme or device Culpable negligence or breach of trust Violating a duty imposed by law or by the terms of a listing agreement; aided, assisted or conspired with another; or formed an intent, design or scheme to engage in such misconduct and committed an overt act in furtherance of such intent, design or scheme	(c)	$1,000 to $2,500 administrative fine and 30-day suspension to revocation	(c) $2,500 to $5,000 administrative fine and 6-month suspension to revocation

FIGURE 2.3 FREC Disciplinary Guidelines as of August 31, 2010 (continued)

Violation		Penalty Range	
		First Violation	Second and Subsequent Violations
(d)	Section 475.25(1)(c), F.S. False, deceptive, or misleading advertising	(d) $250 to $1,000 administrative fine and 30- to 90-day suspension	(d) $1,000 to $5,000 administrative fine and 90-day suspension to revocation
(e)	Section 475.25(1)(d), F.S. Failed to account or deliver to any person as required by agreement or law, escrowed property	(e) $250 to $1,000 administrative fine and suspension to revocation	(e) $1,000 to $5,000 administrative fine and suspension to revocation
(f)	Section 475.25(1)(e), F.S. Violated any rule or order or provision under Chapters 475 and 455, F.S.	(f) $250 to $1,000 administrative fine and suspension to revocation	(f) $1,000 to $5,000 administrative fine and suspension to revocation
(g)	Section 475.25(1)(f), F.S. Convicted or found guilty of a crime related to real estate or involving moral turpitude or fraudulent or dishonest dealing	(g) $250 to $1,000 administrative fine and 30-day suspension to revocation	(g) $1,000 to $5,000 administrative fine and suspension to revocation
(h)	Section 475.25(1)(g), F.S. Has license disciplined or acted against or an application denied by another jurisdiction	(h) $250 to $1,000 administrative fine and 30-day suspension to revocation	(h) $1,000 to $5,000 administrative fine and suspension to revocation
(i)	Section 475.25(1)(h), F.S. Has shared a commission with or paid a fee to a person not properly licensed under Chapter 475, F.S.	(i) $250 to $1,000 administrative fine and 30-day suspension to revocation	(i) $1,000 to $5,000 administrative fine and suspension to revocation
(j)	Section 475.25(1)(i), F.S. Impairment by drunkenness, or use of drugs or temporary mental derangement	(j) Suspension for the period of incapacity	(j) Suspension for the period of incapacity
(k)	Section 475.25(1)(j), F.S. Rendered an opinion that the title to property sold is good or merchantable when not based on opinion of a licensed attorney or has failed to advise prospective buyer to consult an attorney on the merchantability of title or to obtain title insurance	(k) $250 to $1,000 administrative fine and 30-day suspension to revocation	(k) $1,000 to $5,000 administrative fine and suspension to revocation

FIGURE 2.3 FREC Disciplinary Guidelines as of August 31, 2010 (continued)

	Violation		First Violation		Second and Subsequent Violations
			Penalty Range		
(l)	Section 475.25(l)(k), F.S. Has failed, if a broker, to deposit any money in an escrow account immediately upon receipt until disbursement is properly authorized. Has failed, if a sales associate, to place any money to be escrowed with his registered employer	(l)	$250 to $1,000 administrative fine and 30-day suspension to revocation	(l)	$1,000 to $5,000 administrative fine and suspension to revocation
(m)	Section 475.25(1)(l), F.S. Has made or filed a report or record which the licensee knows to be false or willfully failed to file a report or record or willfully impeded such filing as required by State or Federal Law	(m)	$250 to $1,000 administrative fine and 30-day suspension to revocation	(m)	$1,000 to $5,000 administrative fine and suspension to revocation
(n)	Section 475.25(1)(m), F.S. Obtained a license by fraud, misrepresentation, or concealment	(n)	$250 to $1,000 administrative fine and 30-day suspension to revocation	(n)	$1,000 to $5,000 administrative fine and suspension to revocation
(o)	Section 475.25(1)(n), F.S. Confined in jail, prison, or mental institution; or through mental disease can no longer practice with skill and safety	(o)	$250 to $1,000 administrative fine and suspension to revocation	(o)	$1,000 to $5,000 administrative fine and suspension to revocation
(p)	Section 475.25(1)(o), F.S. Guilty for the second time of misconduct in the practice of real estate that demonstrates incompetent, dishonest, or negligent dealings with investors	(p)	$1,000 to $5,000 administrative fine and a 1-year suspension to revocation	(p)	Revocation
(q)	Section 475.25(1)(p), F.S. Failed to give Commission 30-day written notice after a guilty or nolo contendere plea or convicted of any felony	(q)	$500 to $1,000 administrative fine and suspension to revocation	(q)	$1,000 to $5,000 administrative fine and suspension to revocation

FIGURE 2.3 FREC Disciplinary Guidelines as of August 31, 2010 (continued)					
Violation			**Penalty Range**		
			First Violation		**Second and Subsequent Violations**
(r)	Section 475.25(1)(r), F.S. Failed to follow the requirements of a written listing agreement	(r)	$250 to $1,000 administrative fine and suspension to revocation	(r)	$1,000 to $5,000 administrative fine and suspension to revocation
(s)	Section 475.25(1)(s), F.S. Has had a registration suspended, revoked, or otherwise acted against in any jurisdiction	(s)	$250 to $1,000 administrative fine and 60-day suspension to revocation	(s)	$1,000 to $5,000 administrative fine and suspension to revocation
(t)	Section 475.25(1)(t), F.S. Violated the Uniform Standards of Professional Appraisal Practice as defined in Section 475.611, F.S.	(t)	$250 to $1,000 administrative fine and 30-day suspension to revocation	(t)	$1,000 to $5,000 administrative fine and suspension to revocation
(u)	Section 475.25(1)(u), F.S. Has failed, if a broker, to direct, control, or manage a broker associate or sales associate employed by such broker	(u)	$250 to $1,000 administrative fine and suspension to revocation	(u)	$1,000 to $5,000 administrative fine and suspension to revocation
(v)	Section 475.25(1)(v), F.S. Has failed, if a broker, to review the brokerage's trust accounting procedures in order to ensure compliance with this chapter	(v)	$250 to $2,500 administrative fine and suspension to revocation	(v)	$1,000 to $5,000 administrative fine and suspension to revocation
(w)	(w) Section 475.42(1)(a), F.S. Practice without a valid and current license	(w)	$250 to $2,500 administrative fine and suspension to revocation	(w)	$1,000 to $5,000 administrative fine and suspension to revocation
(x)	Section 475.42(1)(b), F.S. Practicing beyond scope as a sales associate	(x)	$250 to $1,000 administrative fine and suspension to revocation	(x)	$1,000 to $5,000 administrative fine and suspension to revocation
(y)	Section 475.42(1)(c), F.S. Broker employs a sales associate who is not the holder of a valid and current license	(y)	$250 to $1,000 administrative fine and suspension to revocation	(y)	$1,000 to $5,000 administrative fine and suspension to revocation

FIGURE 2.3 FREC Disciplinary Guidelines as of August 31, 2010 (continued)

	Violation		Penalty Range		
			First Violation		Second and Subsequent Violations
(z)	Section 475.42(1)(d), F.S. A sales associate shall not collect any money in connection with any real estate brokerage transaction except in the name of the employer	(z)	$250 to $1,000 administrative fine and suspension to revocation	(z)	$1,000 to $5,000 administrative fine and suspension to revocation
(aa)	Section 475.42(1)(e), F.S. A violation of any order or rule of the Commission	(aa)	$250 to $1,000 administrative fine and 30-day suspension to 5-year suspension	(aa)	$1,000 to $5,000 administrative fine and suspension to revocation
(bb)	(bb) Section 475.42(1)(g), F.S. Makes false affidavit or affirmation or false testimony before the Commission	(bb)	$250 to $1,000 administrative fine and suspension to revocation	(bb)	$1,000 to $5,000 administrative fine and suspension to revocation
(cc)	Section 475.42(1)(h), F.S. Fails to comply with subpoena	(cc)	$250 to $1,000 administrative fine and suspension	(cc)	$1,000 to $5,000 administrative fine and suspension to revocation
(dd)	Section 475.42(1)(i), F.S. Obstructs or hinders the enforcement of Chapter 475, F.S.	(dd)	$250 to $1,000 administrative fine and suspension to revocation	(dd)	$1,000 to $5,000 administrative fine and suspension to revocation
(ee)	Section 475.42(1)(j), F.S. No broker or sales associate shall place upon the public records any false, void, or unauthorized information that affects the title or encumbers any real property	(ee)	$250 to $2,500 administrative fine and suspension to revocation	(ee)	$1,000 to $5,000 administrative fine and suspension to revocation
(ff)	Section 475.42(1)(k), F.S. Failed to register trade name with the Commission	(ff)	$250 to $1,000 administrative fine	(ff)	$1,000 to $5,000 administrative fine and suspension to revocation
(gg)	Section 475.42(1)(l), F.S. No person shall knowingly conceal information relating to violations of Chapter 475, F.S.	(gg)	$250 to $1,000 administrative fine and suspension	(gg)	$1,000 to $5,000 administrative fine and suspension to revocation

FIGURE 2.3 FREC Disciplinary Guidelines as of August 31, 2010 (continued)

Violation		Penalty Range			
			First Violation		Second and Subsequent Violations
(hh)	Section 475.42(1)(m), F.S. Fails to have a current license as a broker or sales associate while listing or selling one or more timeshare periods per year	(hh)	$250 to $1,000 administrative fine and suspension	(hh)	$1,000 to $5,000 administrative fine and suspension to revocation
(ii)	Section 475.42(1)(n), F.S. Licensee fails to disclose all material aspects of the resale of timeshare period or timeshare plan and the rights and obligations of both buyer or seller	(ii)	$250 to $1,000 administrative fine and suspension	(ii)	$1,000 to $5,000 administrative fine and suspension to revocation
(jj)	Section 475.42(1)(o), F.S. Publication of false or misleading information; promotion of sales, leases, and rentals	(jj)	$250 to $1,000 administrative fine and suspension to revocation	(jj)	$1,000 to $5,000 administrative fine and suspension to revocation
(kk)	Section 475.451, F.S. School teaching real estate practice fails to obtain a permit from the department and does not abide by regulations of Chapter 475, F.S., and rules adopted by the Commission	(kk)	$250 to $1,000 administrative fine and suspension	(kk)	$1,000 to $5,000 administrative fine and suspension to revocation
(ll)	Section 475.453, F.S. Broker or sales associate participates in any rental information transaction that fails to follow the guidelines adopted by the Commission and Chapter 475, F.S.	(ll)	$250 to $1,000 administrative fine and suspension	(ll)	$1,000 to $5,000 administrative fine and 90-day suspension to revocation
(mm)	Section 475.5015, F.S. Failure to keep and make available to the department such books, accounts, and records as will enable the department to determine whether the broker is in compliance with the provisions of this chapter	(mm)	$250 to $1,000 administrative fine and suspension to revocation	(mm)	$1,000 to $5,000 administrative fine and 90-day suspension to revocation

FIGURE 2.3 FREC Disciplinary Guidelines as of August 31, 2010 (continued)

	Violation		Penalty Range		
			First Violation		Second and Subsequent Violations
(nn)	Section 455.227(1)(s), F.S. Failing to comply with the educational course requirements for domestic violence	(nn)	$250 to $1,000 administrative fine and suspension to revocation	(nn)	$1,000 to $5,000 administrative fine and suspension to revocation
(oo)	Section 455.227(1)(t), F.S. Failing to report in writing to the Commission within 30 days after the licensee is convicted or found guilty of, or entered a plea of nolo contendere or guilty to, regardless of adjudication, a crime in any jurisdiction	(oo)	$250 to $1,000 administrative fine and suspension to revocation	(oo)	$1,000 to $5,000 administrative fine and suspension to revocation
(pp)	Section 455.227(1)(u), F.S. Termination from a treatment program for impaired practitioners as described in Section 456.076 for failure to comply, without good cause, with the terms of the monitoring or treatment contract entered into by the licensee or failing to successfully complete a drug or alcohol treatment program	(pp)	$250 to $1,000 administrative fine and suspension to revocation	(pp)	$1,000 to $5,000 administrative fine and suspension to revocation

(4)(a) When either the Petitioner or Respondent is able to demonstrate aggravating or mitigating circumstances to the Commission in a Section 120.57(2), F.S., hearing or to a Division of Administrative Hearings hearing officer in a Section 120.57(1), F.S., hearing by clear and convincing evidence, the Commission or hearing officer shall be entitled to deviate from the above guidelines in imposing or recommending discipline, respectively, upon a licensee.

Whenever the Petitioner or Respondent intends to introduce such evidence to the Commission in a Section 120.57(2), F.S., hearing, advance notice of no less than seven (7) days shall be given to the other party or else the evidence can be properly excluded by the Commission.

(b) Aggravating or mitigating circumstances may include, but are not limited to, the following:
1. The degree of harm to the consumer or public.
2. The number of counts in the Administrative Complaint.
3. The disciplinary history of the licensee.
4. The status of the licensee at the time the offense was committed.
5. The degree of financial hardship incurred by a licensee as a result of the imposition of a fine or suspension of the license.
6. Violation of the provision of Chapter 475, F.S., wherein a letter of guidance as provided in Section 455.225(4), F.S., previously has been issued to the licensee.

Case Study

I KNOW NOTHING . . .

- **Facts:** In March, a Kissimmee real estate broker contracted with a Wisconsin resident to manage his property. He gave the broker a $500 deposit as a "management reserve balance." The broker was to collect the rent, pay any needed expenses, and remit the balance to the owner. The broker collected $2,525.29 from the tenants. The money was never sent to the owner. The broker told the owner there had been an "accounting breakdown" and promised to make an interim payment the following week but never made the payment. The owner terminated the management contract and the broker promised to send a final accounting "as soon as possible."

In June, the broker contracted with an investor to manage her property in Kissimmee. The broker collected rents but never forwarded money to the investor. Months later, when questioned by the investor, the broker accepted the investor's termination of the management contract, confessing he had never been involved in property management or accounting matters.

Another investor had similar problems in securing a return of $1,000 in "start-up of utility costs." After many calls, letters, and attorney's demands, the investor received a refund.

A department investigator interviewed the broker, but the broker was unable to address the specifics of the complaints. He stated that his wife and son actually ran the business and that they had "poor accounting practices, overspent, and ran out of the money." The investigator was unable to determine whether the broker had paid the funds due to each owner.

The administrative law judge determined that the facts stated by the Department investigator were true.

- **Questions**

1. Did the broker violate the Florida law?

   _____

   _____

2. What sections of Chapter 475, F.S., did the broker violate?

   _____

   _____

3. What should the broker's punishment be?

   _____

   _____

- **Determination of Violation:** The administrative law judge found the broker had violated Sections 475.25(1)(b) and (e) being guilty of "fraud, misrepresentation, culpable negligence, or breach of trust . . . has failed to account and deliver . . . has failed to immediately place funds into an escrow account . . . and has commingled escrow funds. Section 475.5015 requires brokers to keep and make available such books, accounts, and records . . . for at least five years . . . to determine whether broker is in compliance with this chapter."

- **Penalty:** The Administrative Law Judge recommended a $1,000 fine, a two-year suspension, and a requirement to complete the 45-hour sales associate post-licensure course. The Florida Real Estate Commission entered a Final Order affirming the ALJ's recommended order and added an order that the respondent make restitution to the former clients.

Chapter **3**

Other State and Federal Laws Affecting Real Estate

In This Chapter

Condominium Act ● Vacation and time-share plans ● Homeowners' association disclosure ● Community Association Management Act ● Ad valorem tax disclosure ● Amendment 1 regarding property tax relief ● Radon Gas Protection Act ● Local Government Comprehensive Planning Act ● Construction laws relating to unlicensed activity and building code violations ● Federal laws affecting real estate ● The national and state do-not-call registries ● The CAN-SPAM Act ● Junk Fax Prevention Act ● Federal income taxes affecting real estate

Your Quick Reference Guide to the Major Changes in Other State and Federal Laws	**Important changes you should carefully review:** ● Condominium buyers must be given the most recent year-end financial statement. ● Sellers must provide condominium association's Question and Answer Sheet. ● Condominium buyers must be given a governance form. ● Condominium owners who are more than 90 days in arrear on HOA fees may be denied access to amenities. ● The Florida Land Sales Practices Law was deleted. ● Contracts for properties that require membership in a community association must contain language that gives buyers three days to void contracts after receiving the homeowners' association disclosure. ● Property tax disclosure must be made to buyers before the buyer signs a contract. ● Amendment 1 to the Florida Constitution gives property tax relief to homeowners, investors, and business owners. ● Homeowners pay no income taxes on mortgage debt forgiveness.

Learning Objectives

When you have completed this chapter, you should be able to:

- list the time periods for rescission of a purchase contract for new and resale condominiums,

- describe the disclosure that must be on a time-share resale listing agreement,

- list the disclosures necessary when a licensee sells a resale time-share period,

- itemize the factors that would require a person to get a community association manager's license,

- describe the disclosure requirements of the Radon Gas Protection Act,

- describe the process by which a homeowner may exclude the gain on the sale of a personal residence, and

- list the three requirements to be an independent contractor.

CONDOMINIUM ACT (CHAPTER 718, F.S.)

Some describe the concept of the condominium as a "cube in the sky." The cube has a specific legal description, much like a lot-and-block description in a subdivision. The buyer of a condominium purchases title to a unit, usually in fee simple. The owner's exclusive ownership generally extends to the inside of the wall coverings of the condo and includes a proportional share of the common elements. (See Figure 3.1.) The cube rests on a structure that is a common element along with the land and other facilities. Each unit can be bought, sold, leased, or mortgaged. Real estate taxes are separately assessed on each unit.

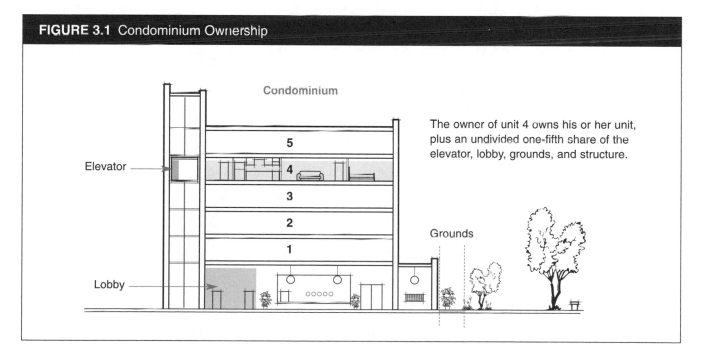

FIGURE 3.1 Condominium Ownership

Source: *Modern Real Estate Practice*, 17th Edition, by Galaty, Allaway, and Kyle. Dearborn Real Estate Education, Chicago, 2006.

The Florida Condominium Act prescribes the process by which condominiums are created, marketed, and operated. It defines common elements, describes the maintenance and assessment of common expenses, and requires full disclosure of information before the sale of the property. Strong controls govern advance payments and deposits. Developers must warrant the improvements for three years after completion of construction. For residential condominiums established after April 1, 1992, each unit's share of common elements maintenance must be related to the unit's total square footage or on an equal fractional basis.

 New

The Division of Florida Condominiums, Timeshares, and Mobile Homes (recent name change) of the Department of Business and Professional Regulation (DBPR) is the agency charged with carrying out the law.

Recent changes to Chapter 718, F.S. include the following:

- The requirement that individual unit owners carry hazard insurance was repealed.
- Investors who purchase blocks of distressed condos are not considered "developers" nor do they take on developers' responsibilities or liabilities.
- Condo associations may now decide whether or not to retrofit a building with sprinkler systems.
- The requirement of mandatory retrofits of sprinkler systems in condos over 75 feet high was repealed.
- Lenders are required to pay more in past-due assessments on foreclosed properties.
- Associations may deny owners or occupants the use of common areas and recreational amenities when the owner is more than 90 days delinquent in paying financial obligations due to the association.
- Associations may divert rent paid by a tenant and use it to pay delinquent assessments owed by that unit's owner.
- A mandate that any amendment to the condominium association's bylaws that restricts a unit owner's rights relating to the rental of units applies only to those unit owners who consent to the amendment and unit owners who purchase their units after the effective date of that amendment. This was a response to court decisions allowing associations to restrict rentals by majority vote.

Buyers may rescind a purchase contract within 15 days for a new condominium or three business days for a resale unit. The time period begins when the buyer signs the contract or is given the required condominium documents, whichever is later. The required documents include the declaration of condominiums, articles of incorporation, bylaws, rules of the association, the condominium association's question and answer sheet, a copy of the most recent year-end financial statement, and a governance form describing the rights and responsibilities of associations and condominium owners.

PROGRESS QUIZ

14. Which condominium disclosure document(s) must be provided to prospective buyers?
    a. Condominium association financial statements for the previous five years
    b. Phase I environmental assessment
    c. Lead-based paint hazard disclosure for units built after 1978
    d. A governance form

IN PRACTICE

Get Relevant Condo Information at Time of Listing

When you are listing a condominium, gather all documents required by the Condominium Act so you'll be ready to give them to the buyer when the parties form a contract.

When you're working with the buyer, you should request information about:

- the dates of recent capital improvements,
- a list of planned capital improvements and the estimated costs of each, and
- a breakdown of how existing and future reserves are allocated.

This information, while not specifically required by the act, is important so that your buyer can evaluate the likelihood of required special assessments to cover capital expenditures or inadequate reserves.

FLORIDA LAND SALES PRACTICES ACT DELETED

 New

The Florida Land Sales Practices Act (Chapter 498, F.S.) was deleted effective July 1, 2008, by the legislature. The Act required developers of 50 or more lots to register with DBPR and to provide buyers with a 7-day right of rescission on property purchases. It was felt that the federal statute was sufficient protection for consumers.

Under the Interstate Land Sales Full Disclosure Act, developers of 25 or more lots must disclose all relevant information in a *property report*, and developers must register subdivisions with 100 or more lots.

VACATION AND TIME-SHARE PLANS (CHAPTER 721, F.S.)

The Florida Real Estate Timesharing Act (FRETSA) prescribes the procedures for the creation, sale, exchange, promotion, and operation of time-share plans. The Division of Florida Condominiums, Timeshares, and Mobile Homes, DBPR, administers the law.

Disclosure Required When Listing a Resale Time-Share Period

When listing a resale time-share period, a licensee must disclose in the listing agreement and in all advertising materials that there is no guarantee that the time-share can be sold at a particular price or within any particular time. Other disclosures are required, including the amount of fees, the term of agreement, promotional efforts if any advance fee is to be paid, and a description of the service to be provided by the broker.

Disclosures Required When Selling a Resale Time-Share Period

Licensees must disclose in the purchase contract the current year's assessment and the fact that it may be increased from time to time.

If ad valorem real property taxes are not included in the current year's assessment for common expenses, the licensee must include the amount of taxes as well as information that failure to pay the taxes may result in loss of the ownership rights.

Disclosures Required When Selling New Time-Share Units

Licensees must have statutory wording in the purchase contract that allows the buyer ten days to cancel the contract with no penalty. Another disclosure alerts the buyer that the property should be purchased as a "leisure-time activity" rather than an investment for appreciation.

If a licensee fails to disclose all material aspects of a time-share sale, or fails to have a current license as a broker or sales associate while listing or selling one or more time-share periods per year, the recommended FREC penalty is revocation.

In 2009, the Florida Attorney General reported that in 2009 there were more consumer complaints about time-share resale companies than complaints about mortgage fraud. The most common problems involved time-share resale companies that charged time-share sellers advance fees of up to $2,000, with a promise that a buyer has been lined up. No sale is made, but the money is not refunded despite promises from the resale company. The attorney general's office has reached settlements with seven resale companies for about $1.6 million in customer refunds.

HOMEOWNERS' ASSOCIATION DISCLOSURE (CHAPTER 720, F.S.)

Some homebuyers in Florida have been surprised shortly after the purchase when they discover that they must pay dues to a *community association* or that there are restrictive covenants that affect the use and occupancy of the property. Developers or owners of the parcel must disclose the following before the buyer signs a purchase contract:

- That the property owner must be a member of the community association
- That recorded covenants govern the use and occupancy of the property
- That the property owner is obligated to pay an assessment to the association, and the failure to pay the assessment could result in a lien being placed on the property
- Any land-use or recreation fees and the amounts of the obligations

Any contract or agreement for sale must refer to and incorporate the disclosure summary and shall include, in prominent language, a statement that the potential buyer should not sign the contract or agreement before having received and read the disclosure summary required by this section.

IN PRACTICE

Get Restrictive Covenants on the Property Early

Even though the disclosure requirement applies only to those community associations that require membership, it is good practice to obtain the appropriate deed restrictions or restrictive covenants on a property when you list it, or during contract negotiations. If the documents are not available when the contract is being negotiated, put a contingency in the contract allowing the buyer a specific number of days to review the restrictions. Some title insurance companies have the covenants available for licensees on their Web sites.

In addition, check out *www.condocerts.com* for many noncertified association documents.

Forms to Go

Only properties that require membership in a community association are covered by the disclosure law. The new disclosure summary is in the Forms-To-Go section.

Each contract entered into for the sale of property governed by covenants subject to disclosure required by this section must contain in conspicuous type a clause that states:

> IF THE DISCLOSURE SUMMARY REQUIRED BY SECTION 720.401, FLORIDA STATUTES, HAS NOT BEEN PROVIDED TO THE PROSPECTIVE PURCHASER BEFORE EXECUTING THIS CONTRACT FOR SALE, THIS CONTRACT IS VOIDABLE BY BUYER BY DELIVERING TO SELLER OR SELLER'S AGENT WRITTEN NOTICE OF THE BUYER'S INTENTION TO CANCEL WITHIN 3 DAYS AFTER RECEIPT OF THE DISCLOSURE SUMMARY OR PRIOR TO CLOSING, WHICHEVER OCCURS FIRST. ANY PURPORTED WAIVER OF THIS VOIDABILITY RIGHT HAS NO EFFECT. BUYER'S RIGHT TO VOID THIS CONTRACT SHALL TERMINATE AT CLOSING.

A contract that does not conform to the requirements of this subsection is voidable at the option of the purchaser within three days, or prior to closing, whichever comes first.

This section does not apply to any associations regulated as Condominiums (Chapter 718), Cooperatives (Chapter 719), Vacation and Timesharing (Chapter 721), or Mobile Home Park Lots (Chapter 723), or to a subdivider registered under the Land Sales Act (Chapter 498). It also does not apply if disclosure regarding the association is otherwise made in connection with the requirements of those chapters.

COMMUNITY ASSOCIATION MANAGEMENT ACT (CHAPTER 468, F.S.)

The Community Association Management Act requires that certain community association managers obtain a license from the DBPR. A community association is defined as "a residential homeowners' association in which membership is a condition of ownership of a unit in a *planned unit development*, or of a lot for a home, mobile home, town house, villa, condominium, cooperative, or other residential unit that is part of a residential development, and that is authorized to impose a fee that may become a lien on the parcel."

It's a community association if it has ten or more units or a budget greater than $100,000.

The term *community association* under this law includes any association that has ten or more units or has an annual budget greater than $100,000. A community association manager must be licensed to perform the following functions for compensation: control or disburse funds, prepare budgets or other financial documents, send notices of meetings or conduct meetings, and coordinate maintenance and other services for the association. This law does not affect apartment properties and other commercial properties.

The law applies only to managers of residential homeowners' associations. Licenses are issued to individuals, not to companies or corporations. To obtain a community association manager's license, an individual must apply to DBPR's Division of Florida Condominiums, Timeshares, and Mobile Homes, pay appropriate fees, be of good moral character, successfully pass a prelicensing course that does not exceed 24 classroom hours, and pass a state examination. A community association manager may not perform real estate services outside the scope of association management unless that person has a real estate license.

AD VALOREM TAX DISCLOSURE (CHAPTER 689, F.S.)

The Save Our Homes Amendment to the Florida Constitution limits the annual increases in the assessed value of a homestead property. The assessment can increase annually by 3 percent or the percentage of increase in the consumer price index, whichever is less. When the property is sold, it is reassessed at full market value. Many buyers are shocked when their first tax bill is much higher than they expected.

Before the buyer signs a contract to purchase, Florida real estate licensees must give a property tax disclosure that includes the following wording:

PROPERTY TAX DISCLOSURE SUMMARY

BUYER SHOULD NOT RELY ON THE SELLER'S CURRENT PROPERTY TAXES AS THE AMOUNT OF PROPERTY TAXES THAT THE BUYER MAY BE OBLIGATED TO PAY IN THE YEAR SUBSEQUENT TO PURCHASE. A CHANGE OF OWNERSHIP OR PROPERTY IMPROVEMENTS TRIGGERS REASSESSMENTS OF THE PROPERTY THAT COULD RESULT IN HIGHER PROPERTY TAXES. IF YOU HAVE ANY QUESTIONS CONCERNING VALUATION, CONTACT THE COUNTY PROPERTY APPRAISER'S OFFICE FOR INFORMATION.

Forms to Go

This form is included in the sample Comprehensive Buyer's Disclosures in the Forms-To-Go section.

PROGRESS QUIZ

15. A frequent but unpleasant effect of the Save Our Homes amendment to a new homeowner is
    a. a limitation on the value that can be excluded from a bankruptcy proceeding.
    b. loss of homestead exemption on properties valued over $1,000,000.
    c. the higher water, sewer, and fire protection fees charged by cities and counties.
    d. the shock they experience when their first full year property tax bill is much higher than expected.

AMENDMENT 1 REGARDING PROPERTY TAX RELIEF

New

Amendment 1 to the Florida Constitution provided tax relief in four different areas:

- Increased homestead exemption
- Portability of the "Save Our Homes" benefit
- $25,000 exemption for tangible personal property
- Ten percent annual assessment limitation for non-homestead property

Increased Homestead Exemption

The original $25,000 assessment reduced taxes for all taxing entities. Homeowners who filed for homestead exemptions are entitled to an additional $25,000 exemption on the property's assessed value between $50,000 and $75,000. The exemption reduced the taxable value of the home for tax levied by city and county governments, special assessment districts, water management districts, etc., *but not for local schools.*

Example of Homestead Exemption

Assessed Value of Homestead	Homestead Exemption Available	Value Subject to Property Tax
$25,000	$25,000 base	0
$50,000	$25,000 base	$25,000
$62,000	$25,000 base + $12,000 non-school levies	$25,000
$90,000	$25,000 base + $25,000 non-school levies	$40,000

Remember, the second $25,000 is not exempt from local school taxes.

Portability of the "Save Our Homes" Benefit

Portability of the "Save Our Homes" (SOH) benefit is available for homeowners who had homestead exemptions on their old home after 2006 and who purchase a new homestead. Homeowners can transfer their SOH benefit to a new home if they had the homestead exemption on the old home in either of the previous two years.

The maximum benefit a homeowner can transfer is $500,000. A person who moves to a more expensive home will transfer the dollar amount. A person moving to a less expensive home transfers the percentage value.

Each applicant for the transfer will have to complete Form DR-501T "Transfer of Homestead Assessment Difference" and submit it to the office of the property appraiser in the county where the new homestead is located.

Example of portability to a more expensive home

Just value of old home	$500,000
Accumulated SOH benefit	$250,000
Assessed value of old home	$250,000
Just value of new home	$800,000
Transferred SOH benefit	$250,000
Assessed value of new home	$550,000

Example of portability to a less expensive home

Just value of old home	$500,000
Accumulated SOH benefit	$250,000
Assessed value of old home	$250,000
Just value of new home	$250,000
Transferred SOH benefit	$125,000
Assessed value of new home	$125,000

NOTE: The SOH benefit was 50 percent of the old home's value ($250,000 ÷ $500,000), so the transfer when downsizing is 50 percent of the new home's value ($250,000 × 0.5).

$25,000 Exemption for Tangible Personal Property

Business owners must file their tangible personal property report with the property appraiser by April 1. If the value of the personal property is less than $25,000, the owner will not have to file a return the following year. If the value of personal property is, for example, $60,000, the owner would pay taxes on the assessed value of $35,000 ($60,000 − $25,000).

Ten Percent Annual Assessment Limitation for Non-Homestead Property

All non-homesteaded property assessments may increase no more than 10 percent of the just value of the property in the prior year. Beginning in 2009, owners of property subject to the limitation must apply with the county property appraiser no later than March 1 of each year. The owner's failure to apply will result in the loss of the assessment limitation. This would be a very costly omission on the part of property owners, and care should be taken that this deadline is not missed.

In years when the just value remains the same, it is still possible that the 10 percent increase could be used to change the assessment if the current just value is higher than the prior year's assessment.

PROGRESS QUIZ

16. Sally's house has a current just value of $400,000 when she sells it in March 2009. She has homestead exemption on the property, and the SOH assessed value is $300,000. If she purchases a new homestead that has current just value of $500,000 within two years, the assessed value of the new home will be
    a. $100,000.
    b. $300,000.
    c. $400,000.
    d. $500,000.

RADON GAS PROTECTION ACT (CHAPTER 404.056, F.S.)

Some authorities contend that radon gas is the second most common source of lung cancer in the United States. Radon is produced by uranium in the soil that decays and creates the gas. While radon gas is all around us, it is not usually a problem because of very low concentrations in the atmosphere. When uranium decays under a home, however, the gas seeps into the home through foundation cracks and plumbing lines. Improved building techniques and insulation intended to provide energy-efficient homes have the unintended side effect of trapping the gas inside the home.

Testing is the only way to learn if radon levels are a health hazard. The EPA recommends intervention if testing shows radon levels at four *picocuries* per liter of air. This would be a concentration approximately ten times that of outdoor air. Exposure to radon inside the home can be reduced to an acceptable level by sealing foundation cracks and other openings and performing sub slab depressurization.

An active subslab depressurization (ASD) radon mitigation system consists of drilling a four-inch hole in the slab and fitting it with PVC piping that leads outside the house. A fan pulls air from under the slab to the outside.

Forms to Go

Florida has enacted the Radon Gas Protection Act, which requires disclosure of the characteristics of the gas but does not require an inspection. The wording must be on every lease contract for more than 45 days and on every sales contract, and is part of the Comprehensive Buyer's Disclosures in the Forms-To-Go section.

Web.Link

A Citizen's Guide to Radon, 4th ed. (U.S. EPA): *www.epa.gov/radon/pubs/citguide.html*

LOCAL GOVERNMENT COMPREHENSIVE PLANNING ACT (CHAPTER 163, F.S.)

Every city and county in Florida must prepare a comprehensive plan of land use, with controls that will implement the plan. The comprehensive plan affects nearly every parcel of undeveloped land and many buildings that need renovation or enlargement.

One problem common to high-growth areas is that improvements such as schools, roads, and utilities ("infrastructure") often lag far behind development in the area. A minimum level of infrastructure must be available before development can take place under the requirement of *concurrency*. The 2009 Florida Legislature substantially revised Florida's growth management requirements by creating *concurrency exception* areas that must meet the following three requirements:

 New

- A municipality that qualifies as a "dense urban land area" (generally defined as an area with an average of 1,000 people per square mile of land, or a county with a population of at least 1 million)
- An urban service area that has been adopted into the local comprehensive plan and is located within a county that qualifies as a dense urban land area
- A county that has a population of at least 900,000 and qualifies as a dense urban land area but does not have an urban service area designated in the local comprehensive plan

Transportation concurrency exception areas do not apply to designated transportation concurrency districts located within a county that has a population of at least 1.5 million, or a county that has exempted more than 40 percent of the area inside the urban service area from transportation concurrency for the purpose of urban infill.

The "urban services area" is in or close to a city. Properties outside the urban services area are more difficult to subdivide, with the number of homes per acre restricted, affecting the ability of licensees to market property for development.

The 2009 Florida Legislature exempted new developments located in dense urban land areas from complying with the development of regional impact (DRI) statute.

New

The sweeping changes in the 2009 growth management legislation has been controversial with many citizens charging that the changes will result in traffic gridlock. Real estate licensees who are knowledgeable about the comprehensive plan in their area will be able to competently help sellers and buyers. Most licensees, even after investigating the possible uses of an undeveloped commercial parcel, insert a "land-use contingency" clause into the contract for purchase. In this way, buyers have a right to cancel a contract for property that cannot be used as represented.

Many cities and counties in Florida now require land-use disclosures prior to contracts being signed by the purchaser. Such disclosures may address:

- restrictive covenants for the neighborhood;
- the buyer's responsibility to investigate whether the anticipated land use conforms to comprehensive planning, zoning, building codes, and so on; or
- whether streets and drainage are maintained by the local government or are the responsibility of the homeowner.

CONSTRUCTION LAWS RELATING TO UNLICENSED ACTIVITY AND BUILDING CODE VIOLATIONS

Hiring a Contractor

The contractor's law allows unlicensed persons to perform any work of a minor nature in which the total contract prices for labor, materials, and all other items are less than $1,000. The exemption does not apply if the construction or repairs are part of a larger operation with several bills from the same or a different person for the purposes of evading this limitation. The unlicensed worker may not do work that requires a contractor's license or building permit.

Real estate licensees should be aware that such workers generally do not carry liability insurance or workers' compensation insurance. This could expose the seller or buyer to substantial liability in case of an accident. [489.103(9), F.S.]

Real Estate Licensees' Exemptions from the Contractor's Law

When a licensee, as agent for an owner, contracts for repairs, maintenance, remodeling, or improvements that total more than $5,000, the licensee must either have a contractor's license or employ a contractor. Dividing the work will not avoid this requirement. If the amount is $5,000 or less, however, the licensee is exempt from the contractor's license requirement. When the work requires a licensed contractor, the licensee must hire licensed persons. [489.013(17), F.S.]

Disclosure of Building Code Violations

Sellers who have been cited for building code violations, or have citations pending, must disclose the facts in writing to buyers prior to closing a sale. The disclosure must:

- state the existence and nature of the violations and proceedings;
- provide a copy of the pleadings, notices, and other materials received by the seller; and
- state the buyer's agreement to be liable for correcting the code violation.

Within five days after transfer of the property, the seller must provide the code enforcement agency with the name and address of the new owner, and provide copies of the disclosure notices given to the buyer.

A seller who violates this provision is guilty of fraud. [125.69(2)(d)]

FEDERAL LAWS AFFECTING REAL ESTATE

Comprehensive Environmental Response, Compensation, and Liability Act of 1980

The Comprehensive Environmental Response, Compensation, and Liability Act (CERCLA) is extremely important to landowners, brokers, developers, and operators. CERCLA assigns potential liability for the cleanup of hazardous substances to any "potentially responsible person" (PRP), including:

- present owners and operators of the contaminated site,
- persons who owned or operated the site at the time hazardous substances were located on the site,
- persons who generated hazardous substances on the site, and
- persons who transported hazardous substances to the site.

It is immaterial whether the PRP is aware of the hazardous substance; the liability may be either strict and/or joint and several. Under the strict liability rules, the government need only show that the person falls within the definition of a PRP. Joint and several liability means that one or more persons in a group, or the entire group, may be liable, and that the person or persons sued are responsible for the total costs of cleanup. The amounts are substantial: since the inception of the Superfund law, owners have paid an average of nearly $500,000 for the cleanup of highly contaminated sites.

To reduce the liability under the "innocent landowner defense," the landowner must have, on or before the date of acquisition,

- carried out all appropriate inquiries into the previous ownership and uses of the property consistent with good commercial and customary standards and practices;
- taken reasonable steps to stop any continuing release;
- prevented any threatened future release; and
- prevented or limited any human, environmental, or natural resource exposure to any previously released hazardous substance. [CERCLA Section 9601(35)(B)]

A purchaser who wishes to avoid liability under the statute must do intensive research, usually in the form of an environmental audit. The audit is broken into the following phases to minimize costs:

- Phase I is a basic assessment.
- Phase II follows to investigate specific problems found in Phase I.
- Phase III is the actual cleanup.
- Phase IV is a Land Disposal Restriction (LDR) rule that prohibits the land disposal of hazardous wastes unless the waste meets specific treatment standards.

A Phase I Environmental Site Assessment (ESA) is one requirement to qualify for the innocent landowner defense to CERCLA.

A Phase I ESA is the evaluation of real property to learn if "recognized environmental conditions" (hazardous substances) exist. Among other things, the evaluation consists of the following:

- A review of governmental records regarding environmental conditions on the property and adjacent properties
- Site reconnaissance of the property
- Interviews with the owners, occupants, and local governmental officials
- Reporting on findings and presentation of conclusions, including documented history of the site dating back to 1940, or until the land was undeveloped

If the Phase I assessment shows actual or potential environmental problems, further investigation to determine the extent of the problem will be required in the form of a Phase II assessment.

If the Phase II assessment shows contamination, Phase III describes cleaning up the contamination.

> **IN PRACTICE**
>
> **Be Very Cautious When Listing and Selling Risky Property**
>
> Prepare a list of properties that you and your associates should be very careful about, such as former gas stations, dry-cleaning establishments, or similar properties nearby, as toxic waste often disburses over a wide area.
>
> Describe the law to your sellers so they know they must make full disclosure, and to your buyers that they must make a due-diligence investigation. You, as a real estate licensee, may become liable by failing to make full disclosure of known problems.

 **Web.Link**   CERCLA Superfund Web page: *www.epa.gov/superfund/*

The Coastal Zone Management Act

The Department of Environmental Protection has established Coastal Construction Control Lines (CCCLs) on a county basis along the sandy beaches of the Atlantic Ocean, the Gulf of Mexico, and the Florida Straits. The lines define the portions of the beach-dune systems that are subject to severe fluctuations based on a 100-year storm surge, storm waves, or other predictable weather conditions. Licensees should be aware that each county or municipality may have additional restrictions that will affect land use. Many buyers have bought land that could not be developed as represented by the licensee, exposing the licensee to substantial civil damages and disciplinary action for culpable negligence. Sellers must provide to buyers, at or before closing, an affidavit or a survey delineating the CCCL location. The buyer may waive this requirement in writing.

If a property is partly seaward of the CCCL, the seller must give the buyer a written disclosure statement, either as part of the contract or on a separate form. The seller's failure to deliver the disclosure, affidavit, or survey required by the law does not, however, impair the enforceability of the sale and purchase contract by either party, create any right of rescission by the purchaser, or impair the title to the property. The required disclosure wording is as follows:

> THE PROPERTY BEING PURCHASED MAY BE SUBJECT TO COASTAL EROSION AND TO FEDERAL, STATE, OR LOCAL REGULATIONS THAT GOVERN COASTAL PROPERTY, INCLUDING THE DELINEATION OF THE COASTAL CONSTRUCTION CONTROL LINE, RIGID COASTAL PROTECTION STRUCTURES, BEACH NOURISHMENT, AND THE PROTECTION OF MARINE TURTLES. ADDITIONAL INFORMATION CAN BE OBTAINED FROM THE FLORIDA DEPARTMENT OF ENVIRONMENTAL PROTECTION, INCLUDING WHETHER THERE ARE SIGNIFICANT EROSION CONDITIONS ASSOCIATED WITH THE SHORELINE OF THE PROPERTY BEING PURCHASED.

Web.Link   Federal Coastal Zone Management Act: *www.fws.gov/laws/lawsdigest/coaszon.html*

Federal Residential Lead-Based Paint Hazard Reduction Act

Lead poisoning causes permanent neurological damage and is particularly toxic to children and pregnant women. The effects include IQ reduction, learning disabilities, hyperactivity, and behavioral problems. Household dust from lead-based paint is the most common cause of poisoning. In 1978, the Consumer Product Safety Commission banned the use of lead-based paint for residential use.

This act requires that disclosures be made to purchasers and tenants of residential buildings built before 1978. The law requires that the seller, landlord, and/or the licensee provide the following to the buyer or tenant before the contract is signed:

- A lead hazard information pamphlet
- A disclosure of any known lead-based paint or lead-based paint hazard
- All test results available to the seller or the landlord. If the property is a multi-family property, the owner must disclose whether lead was found in any other units of the property or in common areas such as playgrounds or laundry rooms
- A ten-day period for the buyer (not a tenant) to conduct an inspection (at the buyer's expense)
- The lead warning statement, as shown in the Forms-To-Go section

Forms to Go

Renovations and demolitions of properties built before 1978 can create lead dust and chips that would be harmful to children and adults. Because of this hazard, the Environmental Protection Agency (EPA) issued a rule to prevent lead contamination that was effective April 22, 2010. The rule requires contractors who disturb paint in these properties to be certified and follow specific work practices. To become certified, a renovator must successfully complete an eight-hour training course offered by an accredited training provider. For more information, see the EPA's Lead Information Web site shown below.

Web.Link

U.S. Department of Environmental Protection: Lead Information Center: *www.epa.gov/lead*

Web.Link

HUD Office of Healthy Homes and Lead Hazard Control: *www.hud.gov/offices/lead*

PROGRESS QUIZ

17. What specific disclosure statement must licensees give the buyer when selling or leasing residential buildings built before 1978?
    a. Notice of nonrepresentation
    b. Radon gas disclosure
    c. Lead-based paint hazard disclosure statement
    d. Good-faith estimate of settlement costs

THE NATIONAL AND STATE DO-NOT-CALL REGISTRIES

In 2003, the Federal Communications Commission (FCC), exercising its authority under the Telephone Consumer Protection Act (TCPA), established a National Do Not Call Registry. The registry is a list of phone numbers of consumers who do not want to be contacted by commercial telemarketers. It is managed by the Federal Trade Commission (FTC), the nation's consumer protection agency, and is enforced by the FTC, the FCC, and state officials.

Do-not-call rules cover the sale of goods or services by telephone. Political organizations, charities, telephone surveyors, or companies with which consumers have existing business relationships are exempt from the do-not-call rules. A company may call a consumer, even if that consumer is on the registry, for no more than (unless waived by signature):

- 18 months after that consumer's last purchase, delivery, or payment; or
- three months after that consumer makes an inquiry or submits an application to the company.

If the consumer asks the company not to call again, the company must honor the request.

Accessing the National Do Not Call Registry

Sellers, telemarketers, and other service providers must pay for access to the registry and may register on the FTC Web site. The National Do Not Call Registry may not be used for any purpose other than preventing telemarketing calls to the telephone numbers in the registry. The only consumer information available from the registry is telephone numbers. The numbers are sorted and available by area code. Companies will be able to access as many area codes as desired. For example, they may select all area codes within a certain state.

Any sellers covered by the rule must pay for consumer data in any area code before they call any consumer within that area code, even those consumers whose telephone numbers are not on the registry. The only exceptions are for sellers who call only consumers with whom they have an existing business relationships or written agreements to call and that do not access the National Do Not Call Registry for any other purpose.

A company that is a seller or telemarketer could be in violation of the law for placing any telemarketing calls (even to numbers NOT on the National Do Not Call Registry) if the company has not paid the required fee for access to the registry. Violators may be subject to fines of up to $11,000 for each call placed.

If a seller or telemarketer can show that, as part of its routine business practice, it meets all of the following conditions, it will not be subject to civil penalties or sanctions for mistakenly calling a consumer who has asked for no more calls or for calling a person on the National Do Not Call Registry. To successfully avoid penalties ("safe harbor"), the sellers or telemarketers must demonstrate that:

- they have written procedures to comply with the do-not-call requirements;
- they train their personnel in those procedures;
- they monitor and enforce compliance with these procedures;
- they maintain a company-specific list of telephone numbers that they may not call;
- they access the national registry no more than three months before calling any consumer, and maintain records documenting this process; and
- any call made in violation of the do-not-call rules was the result of an error.

The best source of information about complying with the do-not-call rules is the FTC's Web site. It includes business information about the registry.

 **Web.Link**   Federal Trade Commission: *www.ftc.gov/donotcall*
www.donotcall.gov

Florida's Do-Not-Call Law

Florida continues to enforce its own do-not-call law, and accepts new consumer telephone numbers. The national registry supersedes portions of the Florida law that are less strict. In order to be placed on Florida's do-not-call list, there is an initial fee of $10 for each residential phone number and a $5 annual renewal fee for each number.

 **Web.Link**   Florida's do-not-call program: *www.800helpfla.com/nosales.html*

IN PRACTICE

Review the List and Check It Twice

Before placing a call, you should be sure that the consumer is not on any of the following lists:

- National Do Not Call Registry
- Florida do-not-call list
- Your broker's own in-office list

You can call a FSBO in the national registry if you have a buyer who wants to purchase the property, but may not use the call to discuss listing the property. Florida's law allows you to call a FSBO on the Florida list (if the FSBO is not on the national registry) to solicit a listing.

PROGRESS QUIZ

18. A telemarketer who mistakenly calls a consumer on the Do-Not-Call Registry has "safe harbor" from prosecution unless the company
    a. trains its personnel.
    b. monitors and enforces compliance with these procedures.
    c. maintains a company-specific list of telephone numbers that it may call.
    d. has a pattern of making such calls.

THE CAN-SPAM ACT

The CAN-SPAM Act of 2003 (Controlling the Assault of Non-Solicited Pornography and Marketing Act) establishes requirements for those who send commercial e-mail, spells out penalties for spammers and companies whose products are advertised in spam if they violate the law, and gives consumers the right to ask e-mailers to stop spamming them.

The law makes a distinction between "commercial" e-mail and "transactional or relationship" e-mail. The act covers only "commercial electronic mail messages" and regulates e-mailers whose "primary purpose" is to advertise a commercial product or service.

"Transactional or relationship" messages include situations like e-mails informing sellers about the progress on marketing a listed property or thanking past customers and updating the relationship. As long as these e-mails don't contain false or misleading routing information, they are exempt from most provisions of the act. Informational messages, such as newsletters that don't contain advertisements, are also exempt.

The law bans false or misleading header information, meaning that the "From", "To", and routing information must be correct and identify the person who sent the e-mail. It requires that the e-mail give recipients an opt-out method. It also requires that commercial e-mail be identified as an advertisement and include the sender's valid physical postal address.

The new rules define the "primary purpose" of the rule as commercial if the e-mail is exclusively an advertisement for a commercial product or service, if a reasonable interpretation of the subject line would lead to the conclusion that a message is commercial, or if a "transactional or relationship" message does not appear in whole or in part at the beginning of the message's body text.

The act is enforced by the Federal Trade Commission and the Department of Justice. Each violation is subject to fines of up to $11,000.

IN PRACTICE

Don't Blanket E-mail Other Real Estate Professionals

It is a common practice for sales associates or brokers to e-mail all real estate professionals in the market area information about their listings. This is a commercial advertising message that, unless requested by the other licensees, could be a violation of the CAN-SPAM Act.

Don't e-mail a commercial message to anyone unless it qualifies as a transactional or relationship e-mail.

@ Web.Link

FTC Web site regarding the CAN-SPAM Act: *www.ftc.gov/spam*

JUNK FAX PREVENTION ACT

The person who sends a fax must:

- have an "established business relationship" with the recipient, or written consent from the recipient;
- have voluntarily received the recipient's fax number;
- provide the recipient the right to "opt-out" of getting more faxes; and
- remove the numbers of persons who opt out within 30 days.

Federal law prohibits most unsolicited fax advertisements to any machine, either business or personal. An unsolicited advertisement is defined under the act as "any material advertising the commercial availability or quality of any property, goods, or services which is transmitted to any person without that person's prior express invitation or permission, in writing or otherwise."

An exception to the rules allows faxes to be sent to recipients with whom the sender has an "established business relationship" or EBR.

If the sender had an EBR with the recipient and possessed the recipient's fax number before July 9, 2005 (the date the Junk Fax Prevention Act became law), the sender may send the fax advertisements without demonstrating how the number was obtained.

Opt-Out Notice Requirements

Senders of fax advertisements must provide specified notice and contact information on the fax that allows recipients to opt out of any future faxes from the sender and specify the circumstances under which a request to opt out complies with the act.

The rules provide that it is unlawful to send unsolicited advertisements to any fax machine, including those at both businesses and residences, without the recipient's prior express invitation or permission. Fax advertisements, however, may be sent to recipients with whom the sender has an EBR, as long as the fax number was provided voluntarily by the recipient. Specifically, a fax advertisement may be sent to an EBR customer if the sender also

- obtains the fax number directly from the recipient through, for example, an application, contact information form, or membership renewal form; or

---

Definition of "Established Business Relationship" (EBR)

An EBR is "a prior or existing relationship formed by a voluntary two-way communication between a person or entity and a business or residential subscriber without an exchange of consideration (payment), on the basis of an inquiry, application, or purchase or transaction by the business or residential subscriber regarding products or services offered by such person or entity, which relationship has not been previously terminated by either party."

- obtains the fax number from the recipient's own directory, advertisement, or site on the Internet, unless the recipient has noted on such materials that it does not accept unsolicited advertisements at the fax number in question; or
- has taken reasonable steps to verify that the recipient consented to have the number listed, if obtained from a directory or other source of information compiled by a third party.

To stop unwanted fax advertisements, your opt-out request must

- identify the fax number or numbers to which it relates; and
- be sent to the telephone number, fax number, Web site address, or e-mail address identified on the fax advertisement.

If you change your mind about receiving fax advertisements, you can subsequently grant express permission to receive faxes from a particular sender orally or in writing.

Fax Broadcasters

Often fax advertisements are sent in bulk on behalf of a business or entity by separate companies called "fax broadcasters." Generally, the person or business on whose behalf a fax is sent or whose property, goods, or services are advertised is liable for a violation of the junk fax rules, even if the person or business did not physically send the fax. A fax broadcaster also may be liable if it has a "high degree of involvement" in the sender's fax message, such as supplying the fax numbers to which the message is sent, providing a source of fax numbers, making representations about the legality of faxing to those numbers, or advising about how to comply with the junk fax rules. Also, if a fax broadcaster is "highly involved" in the sender's fax messages, the fax broadcaster must provide its name on the fax.

FEDERAL INCOME TAXES AFFECTING REAL ESTATE

Real estate licensees are not expected to be income tax experts, but should be knowledgeable about basic tax provisions as they relate to real estate transactions. The information in this section helps licensees provide general information about advantages and disadvantages of taking certain actions. A licensee should advise a consumer to seek professional tax advice. This section describes:

- the ability to exclude all or part of the gain from taxes at the time of sale,
- lower capital gains tax rates,
- deductibility of expenses,
- exclusion of taxes on debt forgiveness,
- federal withholding taxes related to foreign sellers,
- reporting cash payments greater than $10,000 to the IRS,
- deducting the home office, and
- independent contractor relationships.

Ability to Exclude All or Part of the Gain from the Sale of a Personal Residence

An individual filer may exclude up to $250,000 of the gain on the sale of a principal residence. Joint filers are entitled to a $500,000 exclusion. The home must be owned and used as a personal residence for a period of two of the past five years to qualify. The two years do not need to be consecutive. There is no limit on the number of times homeowners may use this exclusion.

Example: The Wilsons bought their home in 1982 for $250,000. In 1992, they added a family room, deck, and pool for a total of $50,000. They lived in the home until they sold it for $900,000 this year. Selling costs were $60,000.

Selling price		$900,000
Less selling expenses		– 60,000
Equals net selling price		$840,000
Basis		
Original cost	$250,000	
Plus improvement	+ 50,000	
Equals cost basis		$300,000
Gain on sale ($840,000 – $300,000)		$540,000
Less exclusion on sale of residence		– $500,000
Taxable capital gain		**$40,000**

The exclusion is available only once every two years, but there are several exceptions. Under the old rules, if the home has been held fewer than two years and if the move is job-related or health-related or there were other unforeseen circumstances, the taxpayer was allowed a prorated portion of the exclusion. The IRS ruled that unforeseen circumstances could include:

- divorce, legal separation, or death of a spouse;
- becoming eligible for unemployment compensation;
- a change in employment that makes it impossible to pay the mortgage or basic living expenses;
- multiple births resulting from the same pregnancy;
- damage to the home from a natural disaster, act of war, or terrorism; and
- condemnation, seizure, or involuntary conversion of the property, such as foreclosure.

Capital Gains Tax Rates on Investment Property

Long-term capital gains (property held for more than 12 months) are taxed at a maximum rate of 15 percent (5 percent for persons in the 15 percent ordinary income tax rate). When investment property is sold, any depreciation taken during the holding period is "recaptured" and is taxed at 25 percent.

Example: An apartment property was purchased nine years ago for $300,000. The building represented 80 percent of the total. The property is sold this year for $510,000 with selling costs of $10,000. Depreciation, using a 27½-year life, is approximately $78,545 ($300,000 × 80% ÷ 27.5 × 9 years). What is the tax liability?

To Calculate Taxes on Gain:

Selling price	$510,000
Less selling costs	– 10,000
Amount realized	$500,000
Deduct purchase price	– 300,000
Gain on sale	$200,000
× Tax rate	× 15%
Taxes on gain	**$30,000**

To Calculate Taxes on Depreciation:

Depreciation taken	$78,545
× Recapture rate	× 25%
Taxes on recapture	**$19,636**

Add Taxes on Gain to Taxes on Depreciation:

Taxes on gain	$30,000
Taxes on depreciation	19,636
Total taxes due on sale	**$49,636**

Deductibility of Expenses

Homeowners can deduct payments of interest and property taxes from their income from federal income taxes if they itemize their deductions. For these deductible items to provide a tax benefit, the total of the taxpayer's deductions, including property taxes and mortgage interest, must exceed the standard deduction. For instance, in 2010, the standard deduction was $11,400 for a married couple filing jointly. This amount increases to keep up with inflation each year. Obviously, if tax deductions for interest and property taxes, added to all other deductions, are less than the standard deduction, the couple would not itemize.

Exclusion from Taxation of Mortgage Debt Forgiveness

 New

The Mortgage Forgiveness Debt Relief Act created a window of time during which homeowners need pay no taxes for mortgage debt forgiveness. Previously, if a lender forgave all or part of a mortgage, the borrower was considered to have received income that was taxable. Under the law, a taxpayer may exclude up to $2 million of income from the debt on a principal residence that is forgiven during the years 2007 through 2012. This includes mortgage debt reduced in a mortgage refinance as well as debt forgiven in a foreclosure.

The rule applies only to acquisition indebtedness, which would be funds for the purchase or improvement of the home. Home equity loans not used for improvements do not receive the benefit.

The lender who forgives a mortgage must send the taxpayer a Form 1099C or 1099A that should show the fair market value of the home and the amount of the loan. The difference would normally be the income received. If audited, the taxpayer will have to document that funds were spent for the purchase or improvement of the home.

 Web.Link

U.S. Internal Revenue Service (The Mortgage Forgiveness Debt Relief Act and Debt Cancellation): *www.irs.gov/individuals/article/0,,id=179414,00.html*

Federal Withholding Taxes Related to Foreign Sellers

Under the Foreign Investment in Real Property Tax Act of 1980 (FIRPTA), when a foreign person sells real property, the purchaser may be required to withhold 10 percent of the amount realized (which is usually the sales price). The buyer must find out if the seller is a foreign person, and might wish to get an affidavit of U.S. citizenship if in doubt. If the buyer fails to withhold, he or she may be held liable for the taxes on the sale.

One of the most common exceptions to FIRPTA withholding is that the buyer is not required to withhold tax when purchasing real estate for use as his home and the purchase price is not more than $300,000.

 Web.Link

U.S. Internal Revenue Service (FIRPTA):
www.irs.gov/businesses/small/international/article/0,,id=105000,00.html

Reporting Cash Payments Greater Than $10,000

If a broker receives more than $10,000 in cash for a single real estate transaction, or two or more related transactions, the broker must report the event to the IRS within 15 days on Form 8300. Cash is U.S. or foreign currency. Brokers selling real property need not report funds received by bank check or wire transfer when cash was not physically transferred.

Deducting the Home Office

Many brokers and sales associates work from their homes. If the office is qualified, they may deduct up to $24,000 for the cost of their computers as well as proportionate shares of heating, cooling, and maintenance expenses of the home. To qualify, the home office must be an area used exclusively for business activity, and it must be the principal location used to conduct business or meet with customers. The IRS is very strict in granting the home office deduction and has disallowed the deduction when it determined that a taxpayer kept personal correspondence in the same area used for the business. Because sales associates are furnished an office by the broker, they are not allowed to take home-office deductions. Licensees should seek professional advice or review IRS Publication 587. (See Figure 3.2.)

Independent Contractor Relationships

Most real estate brokerage firms contract with their sales associates to be independent contractors. If the broker meets all requirements, this results in substantial savings, primarily from the employer's share of Social Security taxes, workers' compensation insurance, unemployment taxes, and other fringe benefits. There are three major requirements to qualify for independent contractor status:

- The sales associate must hold a real estate license.
- The sales associate's gross income must be based on production rather than on the number of hours worked.
- The sales associate's work must be done based on a written contract that states, among other things, that the sales associate will not be considered an employee for federal tax purposes.

However, if the broker reimburses the sales associate for business costs such as automobile expenses and pays for business cards, insurance plans, or licensing or board dues, the IRS may determine that the sales associate is an employee. The broker would then be liable for Social Security and Medicare taxes and income taxes.

 **Web.Link**

U.S. Internal Revenue Service: *www.irs.ustreas.gov*

U.S. Internal Revenue Service (Home Office Deduction): *www.irs.gov/newsroom/article/0,,id=108138,00.html*

FIGURE 3.2 Can You Deduct the Business Use of Your Home Expenses?

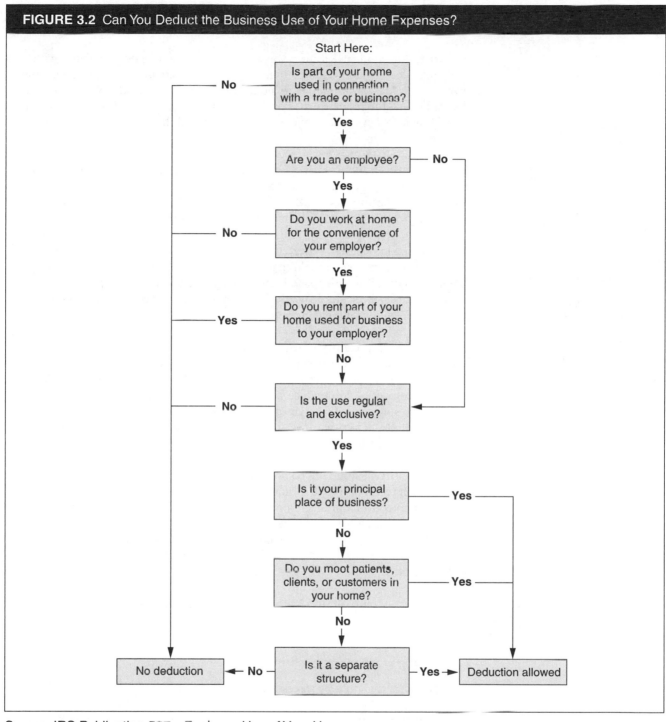

Source: IRS Publication 587—Business Use of Your Home

Case Study

SALES ASSOCIATE DEFRAUDS OWNER

● **Facts:** Respondent Kathryn was an active sales associate associated with a brokerage corporation. Complainant Donald, a resident of Canada, was the owner of residential property in Indian Rocks Beach, Florida. When Donald decided to sell the residence, he contacted Kathryn, who agreed to list the property. Donald believed the home was listed, although he never received a listing agreement.

Because Kathryn had sold her house and needed a place to live, Donald and Kathryn agreed that Kathryn could move into the home and pay rent of $1,400 directly into the owner's bank account monthly. Donald sent a written rental agreement for Kathryn to sign, but it was never returned.

After moving in, Kathryn reported to the owners that the home needed roof and air conditioner repairs. Donald mailed a check for $2,000, which, the investigation later showed, was deposited into Kathryn's personal bank account. Later, Donald sent a check for $500 that was endorsed by Kathryn and cashed by Dave, an air-conditioning contractor.

Donald asked that Kathryn provide a "full disclosure of all bills and receipts, a copy of the real estate agreement, and a signed copy of our lease agreement." Kathryn did not initially respond to the request, but subsequently provided to Donald a copy of a "Job Invoice" from Service Air Systems for a total of $3,003. The invoice states that Kathryn ordered the work. The invoice is marked "Paid in Full, 5/30/96, KM." An investigation found no evidence that Kathryn paid $3,003 for air-conditioning work on Donald's home.

Based on Kathryn's failure to respond to repeated requests for documentation, or to pay the agreed-upon rent, Donald traveled to Florida to resolve the situation. Kathryn agreed to reimburse Donald for $6,500 for the unsupported payments and unpaid rent and to vacate the property. Kathryn vacated the home, but did not make any of the payments. Donald filed a complaint with the DBPR.

● **Questions:**

1. What, if anything, should Kathryn be charged with by the DBPR?

   _____

   _____

2. What penalty should be assessed against Kathryn?

   _____

   _____

● **Determination of Violation:** The administrative law judge found that Kathryn was guilty of fraud, misrepresentation, concealment, false promises, false pretenses, dishonest dealing by trick, scheme, or device, culpable negligence, or breach of trust in any business transaction in this state or any other state, nation, or territory; had violated a duty imposed upon her by law or by the terms of a listing contract, written, oral, express, or implied, in a real estate transaction. She also failed to account and deliver funds entrusted to her by the owner.

● **Penalty:** Upon the recommendation of the administrative law judge, the Florida Real Estate Commission entered a final order revoking Kathryn's license.

Chapter **4**

Real Estate Brokerage Relationships

In This Chapter

Brokerage relationships ● Brokerage Relationship Disclosure Act ● Authorized brokerage relationships ● Disclosure requirements ● Disclosure limitations ● Transaction broker relationship ● Single-agent relationship ● Single-agent duties ● Transitioning from single agent ● No brokerage relationship ● The designated sales associate ● Retaining brokerage relationship disclosure documents

Your Quick Reference Guide to the Major Changes in Florida Brokerage Relationships

Important changes you should carefully review:

● The Transaction Broker Notice requirement has been deleted.

Learning Objectives

When you have completed this chapter, you should be able to:

● distinguish the differences between the duties of single-agent brokers, transaction brokers, and brokers with "no representation" status;

● distinguish between the terms *principal* and *customer;*

● understand the types of real property transactions requiring that licensees disclose the broker's relationship to buyers and sellers;

● list the different disclosure forms a licensee must give to buyers and sellers of residential property and understand the uses of each;

● distinguish between the licensee's fiduciary responsibilities to principals and the general obligations owed to other parties;

● define and explain the term *agency;* and

● describe the fiduciary duties an agent owes to his or her principal.

BROKERAGE RELATIONSHIPS

While the law of agency is clear and straightforward, its application to the real estate brokerage business is quite complex. This chapter updates licensees concerning broker's relationships with parties to transactions and the disclosure requirements of Florida law.

The laws of agency govern the dealings between single-agent brokers and their principals. They are the product of common law, case law, and statute.

BROKERAGE RELATIONSHIP DISCLOSURE ACT

The Brokerage Relationship Disclosure Act is important to licensees in two principal areas:

- It describes the *type of brokerage relationship* a licensee may have with a customer. This section of the law applies to all licensees.
- It requires *disclosure of the brokerage relationship* a licensee has with a customer. This section of the law applies only to licensees dealing in residential property sales.

AUTHORIZED BROKERAGE RELATIONSHIPS

A real estate licensee may have brokerage relationships with potential buyers and sellers, either as single agents or as transaction brokers. It is illegal for a licensee to be a dual agent. A licensee may also work with a customer in a no brokerage relationship.

It is legally presumed that all licensees are operating as transaction brokers unless single-agent or no brokerage relationships are established, in writing, with customers. [475.278(1)(b), F.S.]

The broker determines the type of relationship to have with a buyer or a seller. If a single-agency relationship is established with a residential seller, all licensees in that brokerage firm have single-agent duties to the seller. It is not legal for another sales associate in the firm to represent a buyer or be a transaction broker when showing a buyer that seller's property. A sales associate may not decide the type of relationship without the broker's consent.

After a brokerage relationship has been established, a licensee may change from one brokerage relationship to another. The licensee must make the appropriate disclosure of duties to the principal, and the principal must give written consent before the change. A customer is not required to enter a brokerage relationship with any real estate licensee. [475.278(1)]

All licensees have the legal duties of:

- fair and honest dealing with customers,
- disclosure of known facts that materially affect the value of residential property and that are not readily observable to the buyer, and
- accounting for all funds.

Additional duties are imposed on single agents and transaction brokers.

> **PROGRESS QUIZ**
>
> 19. What brokerage relationship is presumed under Florida law?
>   a. No brokerage relationship
>   b. Transaction broker
>   c. Single agent
>   d. Designated sales associate

DISCLOSURE REQUIREMENTS

Single agents and licensees with no brokerage relationship must disclose their status to customers only in residential real estate sales. *Residential sales* are defined as the sales of:

- improved residential property of four units or less,
- unimproved residential property intended for use as four units or less, and
- agricultural property of ten acres or less.

DISCLOSURE LIMITATIONS

The real estate disclosure requirements of this section do not apply:

- when a licensee knows that the potential seller or buyer is represented by a single agent or a transaction broker;
- when an owner is selling new residential units built by the owner and the circumstances or setting should reasonably inform the potential buyer that the owner's employee or single agent is acting on behalf of the owner, whether because of the location of the sales office or because of office signage or placards or identification badges worn by the owner's employee or single agent;
- to nonresidential transactions;
- to the rental or leasing of real property, unless an option to purchase all or a portion of the property improved with four or fewer residential units is given;
- to a bona fide open house or model home showing that does not involve eliciting confidential information, the execution of a contractual offer or an agreement for representation, or negotiations concerning price, terms, or conditions of a potential sale;
- to unanticipated casual conversations between a licensee and a seller or buyer that do not involve eliciting confidential information, execution of contractual offers or agreements for representation, or negotiations concerning price, terms, or conditions of a potential sale;
- when responding to general factual questions from a potential buyer or seller concerning properties that have been advertised for sale;
- to situations in which a licensee's communications with a potential buyer or seller are limited to providing general factual information, oral or written, about the qualifications, background, and services of the licensee or the licensee's brokerage firm;
- to auctions, appraisals, and dispositions of any interest in business enterprises or business opportunities, except for property with four or fewer residential units; and
- to licensees acting as transaction brokers.

If a licensee will be a single agent, the licensee must provide disclosure before or at the time of entering into a listing agreement or a buyer representative agreement for representation or before the showing of property, whichever occurs first. If a licensee will not be representing a customer in any capacity, the licensee must give the customer a No Brokerage Relationship Notice before showing a property.

There are three different disclosure notices that may be given to buyers or sellers of residential property:

1. Single Agent Relationship
2. Consent to Transition to Transaction Broker
3. No Brokerage Relationship

PROGRESS QUIZ

20. All of the following transactions involving a single agent would require a brokerage relationship disclosure to a customer EXCEPT
    a. a sale of improved property with four units or fewer.
    b. a sale of agricultural property with ten or fewer acres.
    c. leasing residential property.
    d. a sale of an unimproved single-family lot.

TRANSACTION BROKER RELATIONSHIP

Under the law, licensees are presumed to be transaction brokers. A transaction broker provides limited representation to a buyer, a seller, or both in a real estate transaction but does not represent either in a fiduciary capacity. The licensee is not an advocate for either party. The licensee must treat the parties fairly and not work for one party to the detriment of the other. The customer is not the broker's principal and is not responsible for the acts of the licensee.

Transaction Broker Duties

The duties of the transaction broker include the following:

- Dealing honestly and fairly
- Accounting for all funds
- Using skill, care, and diligence in the transaction
- Disclosing all known facts that materially affect the value of residential real property and are not readily observable to the buyer
- Presenting all offers and counteroffers in a timely manner, unless a party has previously directed the licensees otherwise in writing
- Limited confidentiality, unless waived in writing by a party. The transaction broker may *not* reveal to either party the following information:
  - That the seller might accept a price less than the asking or list price
  - That the buyer might pay a price greater than the price submitted in a written offer
  - The motivation of any party for selling or buying property
  - That a seller or buyer will agree to financing terms other than those offered
- Any other information requested by a party to remain confidential
- Any additional duties that are entered into by this or by a separate agreement

Creation of a Transaction Brokerage Relationship

Transaction brokerage relationships can begin in one of two ways:

- The broker chooses to be a transaction broker in all transactions.
- A single-agent broker becomes a transaction broker to facilitate the transaction and to sell one of the firm's listings.

The broker chooses to be a transaction broker in all transactions. Some brokers recognize the increased liability because of the complexities of the disclosure requirements and the need for their sales associates to remember which "hats" they are wearing in specific transactions. Customers and licensees can become confused if the licensee is a single agent for a buyer until showing the firm's own listings and then changes to a transaction broker.

For this reason, many brokers have established the policy that their firm will act as transaction brokers in every situation with every customer. (The only time the policy might change is the rare situation when a customer wishes the broker to have "no brokerage relationship" status.) All licensees in the firm then have the same role in every transaction, reducing the chance the licensees will inadvertently violate their legal duty.

A single agent becomes a transaction broker to facilitate the transaction. The need for a single agent to become a transaction broker frequently occurs when the buyer and seller are working with the same brokerage firm.

Neither party will want to be unrepresented in the transaction, and either might request that the single agent take the middle ground between the parties and become a transaction broker. This status makes it easier for brokers to sell their own listing. The next section describes the steps necessary to change from a single agent to a transaction broker.

Transaction Broker Notice Deleted

 New

The requirement that licensees give customers a Transaction Broker Notice was deleted effective July 1, 2008. The duties of a transaction broker are not eliminated, only the requirement to give the form to the customer.

IN PRACTICE

Nothing in the Law Says You Can't Use It

If you are working as a transaction broker and get a question from a customer about what that status means, you may still use the old form and go over your duties with the customer. The Consent to Transition to Transaction Broker Notice was not changed by the legislation, so the duties of the transaction broker are still clearly spelled out in this form.

PROGRESS QUIZ

21. A transaction broker owes all these duties to the customer EXCEPT
    a. limited confidentiality.
    b. obedience.
    c. skill, care, and diligence.
    d. disclosing all known facts that materially affect the value of residential property.

SINGLE-AGENT RELATIONSHIP

A single agent represents, as a fiduciary, either the buyer or seller *but not both* in the same transaction. Being a single-agent broker does not mean, however, that there must be two brokers in every transaction. For example, a single-agent broker who represents the seller may work with a buyer as a nonrepresentative.

Fiduciary Relationship

A fiduciary relationship is a position of trust and confidence in which the fiduciary is entrusted to manage the property of the principal. The principal relies on the real estate single agent to give skilled and knowledgeable advice and to help negotiate the best transaction in dealings with the customer. Because only a single agency creates a fiduciary relationship, only single agents may call their customers *principals.* Once a single-agent relationship is created, the law requires that the agent place the interests of the principal above the interests of everyone else, including those of the agent. The principal is responsible for the acts of the single agent.

Creation of Single-Agent Relationships

A single-agent relationship results from mutual consent between the principal and the agent. The broker requires only the principal's specific authorization for representation. A single agency is not created simply because a licensee performs a service for a customer. Payment of a commission is not a factor in creating a single-agent relationship. A single agent does not need a written contract or compensation for an agency relationship to exist.

SINGLE-AGENT DUTIES

A single agent owes nine specific duties to a buyer or seller:

- Dealing honestly and fairly
- Loyalty
- Confidentiality
- Obedience
- Full disclosure
- Accounting for all funds
- Skill, care, and diligence in the transaction
- Presenting all offers and counteroffers in a timely manner, unless a party has previously directed the licensee otherwise in writing
- Disclosing all known facts that materially affect the value of residential real property and are not readily observable

Single Agent Notice

The duties of a single agent must be disclosed in writing to a buyer or seller. It may be a separate and distinct disclosure document or part of another document, such as a listing agreement or a buyer's representation agreement. The disclosure must be made either before or at the time of entering into a listing agreement or an agreement for representation or before the showing of property, whichever occurs first. In 2006, the form was changed to remove the "Important Notice" section. The Single Agent Notice is included in the Forms-To-Go section.

 Forms to Go

The notice should be signed. If a principal refuses to sign a Single Agent Notice, the licensee may still work as a single agent for that person but should note on the form that the principal declined to sign.

PROGRESS QUIZ

22. Janice lists the Smiths' home as a single agent on the condition that she remain a single agent throughout the transaction. A buyer calls Janice after she sees an advertisement and wants to see the property. What brokerage status will Janice have with the buyer?
    a. A single-agent relationship
    b. A dual-agent relationship
    c. A transaction broker relationship
    d. No brokerage relationship

TRANSITIONING FROM SINGLE AGENT

When a single agent for one party begins working with a party who is likely to be on the other side of the transaction, it is likely that the agent will change to a transaction broker to treat both parties fairly. The single agent who becomes a transaction broker may not disclose to another party any information gained while a single agent.

Example: Broker James listed the Smiths' house as their single agent. Sally, a licensee in Broker James's office, is working as the single agent for a buyer, Mr. Farley. Mr. Farley becomes interested in the Smiths' house. Because the broker cannot represent both parties (dual agency), the broker obtains the informed written consent of both parties for him to switch to transaction broker status.

Consent to Transition to Transaction Broker Notice

The Consent to Transition to Transaction Broker Notice allows a single agent to change his or her brokerage relationship to that of a transaction broker. It must be provided before or at the time of changing the brokerage relationship from single agent to transaction broker. The Consent to Transition to Transaction Broker Notice is in the Forms-To-Go section.

 Forms to Go

The principal must sign the notice before the single agent may change to transaction broker status. This form may be included in a listing or representation agreement and be authorized at the outset of the single-agent relationship. The single-agent broker must disclose the fact before changing to transaction broker.

In practice, many licensees who are single agents will have the principal sign the Consent to Transition to Transaction Broker Notice when the Single Agent Notice is given. The forms are usually included as part of listing agreements and buyers' representation agreements.

PROGRESS QUIZ

23. A sales associate would be legally able to tell the buyer the seller will take less than the listed price when the sales associate is the
    a. single agent for the seller.
    b. transaction broker for the buyer.
    c. designated sales associate for the seller.
    d. single agent for the buyer.

IN PRACTICE

Switching from Transaction Broker to Single Agent

If you are working with the seller as a transaction broker and the buyer has a single agent who is a strong advocate on how to structure a transaction, you may legally decide to change hats and become a single agent for your seller to give stronger representation. Just make sure disclosures are given to all parties.

NO BROKERAGE RELATIONSHIP

Licensees working with a customer without a brokerage relationship owe the customer the following duties:

- Dealing honestly and fairly
- Disclosing all known facts that materially affect the value of the residential real property that are not readily observable to the buyer
- Accounting for all funds entrusted to the licensee

Occasionally, a single agent for one party in a transaction decides to work with the other party as a nonrepresentative. In fact, before the practice of buyer brokerage became popular, most brokers worked for sellers, and buyers were not represented in the transaction. If a broker does not have a brokerage relationship with a customer, and is a single agent for the other party, the customer is at a disadvantage. It is the duty of the single agent to work diligently for the principal and obtain the best price and terms.

No Brokerage Relationship Notice

A licensee must give a No Brokerage Relationship Notice to the party the licensee works with but does *not* represent. It may be a separate and distinct disclosure document or part of another document, such as a listing agreement or a buyer's representation agreement. The disclosure must be given to all prospective buyers and sellers of residential properties who are not represented by a broker in a transaction-broker or single-agency relationship before showing them. The notice need not be signed. In 2006, the required form was changed to remove the "Important Notice" section at the top. The notice is included in the Forms-To-Go section.

 Forms to Go

Quick Chart of Licensee's Brokerage Relationship Duties

This chart is designed to help you quickly locate the duties depending on your brokerage relationship status.

Single Agent	Transaction Broker	No Brokerage Relationship
Dealing honestly and fairly	Dealing honestly and fairly	Dealing honestly and fairly
Loyalty	Limited confidentiality	Accounting for all funds
Confidentiality	Accounting for all funds	Disclosing all known facts that materially affect value
Obedience	Skill, care, and diligence	
Full disclosure	Presenting all offers	
Accounting for all funds	Disclosing all known facts that materially affect value	
Skill, care, and diligence	Any additional duties	
Presenting all offers		
Disclosing all known facts that materially affect value		

THE DESIGNATED SALES ASSOCIATE

Florida law allows a brokerage firm to designate one sales associate in the firm to act as agent for the buyer (or lessee) and another sales associate in the firm to act as the agent for the seller (or lessor). This status may be used only in a nonresidential transaction. In this status, each *designated sales associate* is an advocate for the party the associate represents in the transaction, and each can actively help in the negotiations. To meet the requirements of the law, buyers and sellers must each have personal assets of at least $1 million, must sign disclosures that each person's assets meet the requirement, and must request this representation status. The licensees must give the parties the Designated Sales Associate Notice and a Single Agent Notice. As a matter of practice, many firms now use a combined form that includes all the required information. A sample notice is shown in the Forms-To-Go section.

Forms to Go

Example: Big Bagels, Inc., is searching for five store locations in Sarasota. It engages Mary Perez of Sarasota Commerce Realty as a single agent because of her knowledge and expertise in the Sarasota fast-food field.

Mary finds a site listed by another sales associate in her firm. Big Bagels, Inc., wants Mary to be its single agent, so the broker appoints Mary as a single agent for Big Bagels, Inc., and Jack as single agent for the seller. They are now designated sales associates.

RETAINING BROKERAGE RELATIONSHIP DISCLOSURE DOCUMENTS

Brokers must keep copies of disclosure notices for all residential transactions that result in written sales contracts for at least five years. It does not matter whether the sales close. DBPR investigators review brokerage relationship disclosure notices during office inspection visits.

PROGRESS QUIZ

24. In a nonresidential transaction, which status allows a broker to appoint one sales associate in a firm to act as single agent for the buyer and one agent in the firm to act as single agent for the seller?
    a. Dual agency
    b. Single agency
    c. Transaction broker
    d. Designated sales associate

25. Required brokerage relationship disclosures must be retained by the broker for how many years?
    a. One
    b. Three
    c. Four
    d. Five

Case Study

PROPERTY MANAGER FAILS TO NOTIFY THE FREC OF A DISPUTE OVER A RENTAL DEPOSIT

● **Facts:** Broker Samuels accepted a $25 application fee and $585 as a holding deposit for a rental unit. If Ms. Markham, the prospective tenant, was deemed qualified, she would receive a lease. The property was taken off the rental market during the credit check period, after which the tenant was approved. Ms. Markham changed her mind about the rental unit and requested a refund of the holding deposit. Broker Samuels sent Ms. Markham a notice of his intent to keep the rental deposit in conformance with Subsection 83.49(3), F.S., and delivered the deposit to the property owner. No notice was sent to the FREC about the dispute over the deposit.

The DBPR charged the broker with failure to account and deliver escrowed property, citing the fact that Ms. Markham never signed a lease, possessed keys, or had the right to occupy the unit.

Broker Samuels countered that Subsection 83.49(3) supersedes Chapter 475 in this regard, that he complied with the appropriate statutes, and that the conflicting demands requirements of Chapter 475, F.S., did not apply.

● **Questions:**

1. Did Broker Samuels violate the law?

   _____

   _____

2. Was Ms. Markham a tenant, and was this a landlord-tenant dispute?

   _____

   _____

3. What, if anything, should Broker Samuels's punishment be?

   _____

   _____

● **Determination of Violation:** The administrative law judge (ALJ) found in favor of Broker Samuels. The ALJ agreed with Samuels's position that the application clearly evidenced the parties' intent to create a landlord and tenant relationship, and the fact that the lease was not executed did not change the nature of the transaction. The ALJ said the evidence failed to show any failure to account or deliver funds, and recommended that the DBPR enter a final order dismissing the administrative complaint against Samuels.

Chapter 5

Property Condition and Inspections

In This Chapter

Required residential property condition disclosures ● Florida court decisions on property disclosure ● Nonresidential property condition disclosures ● Licensees' disclosure duties under the Brokerage Relationship Disclosure Act ● Licensing of Florida home inspectors ● The nuts and bolts of a home inspection ● Inspecting the exterior ● Inspecting the Interior ● Environmental problems

Important changes you should carefully review:

● Florida home inspectors must be licensed.

Learning Objectives

When you have completed this chapter, you should be able to:

● describe the issues settled in *Johnson v. Davis* and *Raynor v. Wise Realty,*

● state the type of property that requires disclosure of known facts that affect the value of property,

● describe how getting the seller to sign a property disclosure statement can benefit both the buyer and the seller,

● describe how insulation effectiveness is measured, and

● list at least three environmental problems in buildings.

REQUIRED RESIDENTIAL PROPERTY CONDITION DISCLOSURES

Real estate licensees and sellers are being held to ever-higher standards of property condition disclosure in residential transactions. This chapter examines required disclosures and details methods of avoiding charges of misrepresentation.

FLORIDA COURT DECISIONS ON PROPERTY DISCLOSURE

Johnson v. Davis

In May of 1982, the Davises contracted to buy the Johnsons' three-year-old home for $310,000. The contract specified that the buyer had the right to have a roof inspection made. Mr. Davis noticed stains on the ceilings in the kitchen and family room and was told by Mr. Johnson that the window had a minor problem and had been repaired, and that the stains were wallpaper glue. Several days later, during a heavy rain and before closing, Mr. Davis discovered water gushing in around the window frame, the ceiling fixtures, and the kitchen stove. Three roofers hired by the Davises said the roof was "slipping," and that only a new $15,000 roof would be watertight. The Davises sued for rescission of contract and a return of all deposits.

The trial court found for the Davises and ordered a return of all deposits. The Third District Court of Appeals affirmed the return of only part of the deposit to the Davises. The Davises appealed to the Florida Supreme Court.

The Supreme Court ruled that the Johnsons knew of and failed to disclose that there had been problems with the roof of the house. The Court also held that the fraudulent misrepresentations made by the Johnsons were not the deciding factor, and even if the Johnsons had not made the statements, there would have been fraudulent concealment. The Court stated: "Accordingly, we hold that where the seller of a home knows of facts materially affecting the value of the property which are not readily observable and are not known to the buyer, the seller is under a duty to disclose them to the buyer."

This landmark case in favor of consumers overturned previous decisions favoring the seller under "caveat emptor." It has had a broad effect in Florida. Chapter 475, F.S., has extended the duty to real estate licensees selling residential property.

Raynor v. Wise Realty

In 1987, the Court ruled in another important case, *Raynor v. Wise Realty*. In that case, the buyer agreed to an "as-is" contract on an older home. The real estate licensee had two wood-destroying organism inspections made, one showing termite infestation and the other showing that the property was clear. The licensee brought the "clear" report to the closing, believing that it did not really matter because of the "as-is" contract. In its decision, the Court ruled that real estate licensees also have duties of disclosure, and the fact that an "as-is" contract exists does not affect that duty.

NONRESIDENTIAL PROPERTY CONDITION DISCLOSURES

Because buyers of investment property are considered more "sophisticated" than homebuyers, the laws are not as protective when nonresidential property is sold. In South Florida, a subdivision developer sued the seller, who knew about but failed to disclose soil pollution. Toxic waste made the property unfit for its intended use. The local court dismissed the suit, saying the *Johnson v. Davis* decision requiring disclosure of property condition clearly applied to residential property only.

IN PRACTICE

How Much Should You Disclose about Commercial Property Defects?

If you sell commercial property, you should exercise caution when you are aware of property defects. While Chapter 475, F.S., requires disclosure only when selling residential property, you should consider the potential damage to your reputation by failing to disclose major problems that may result in substantial damage to the buyer. While the best course of action is full disclosure, a seller may allege that you violated a fiduciary duty by making a disclosure that was not required. Therefore, before making such disclosures, you get the informed consent of the seller. If the seller refuses to allow the disclosure, you must then decide whether to proceed under those instructions or withdraw from the transaction. This is particularly important under CERCLA laws. If you don't disclose problems, you may become liable for all or part of the cleanup costs.

LICENSEES' DISCLOSURE DUTIES UNDER THE BROKERAGE RELATIONSHIP DISCLOSURE ACT

The 1997 Brokerage Relationship Disclosure Act (Chapter 475.2701, F.S.) included the duty for all licensees in a residential transaction to disclose "all known facts that materially affect the value of residential real property and are not readily observable to the buyer." The law is intended to ensure a standard of quality that protects consumers and builds their confidence when purchasing properties.

Misrepresentation and Condition Disclosure

The Chapter 475 modernization repealed the requirement that a licensee, on written request of any party to a transaction, furnish copies of any termite and roof inspection report. This change was made because the law requires that a licensee, even without such a written request, disclose any material defects affecting the value of residential property.

IN PRACTICE

Steps You Should Take to Avoid Claims of Misrepresentation

Some practical steps a real estate agent can take to decrease the risk of misrepresentation claims follow:

1. Question the seller thoroughly regarding the property. While it is not a legal requirement, licensees should use a Seller's Property Disclosure Statement. When a buyer becomes interested in the property, the buyer should receive a copy of the seller's disclosure statement and sign the receipt for the broker's records. This is one of the most effective ways to reduce a licensee's liability.
2. Make a general visual inspection of the property and ask the seller questions if there is apparent evidence of a defect.
3. Don't make statements to a buyer that are not based on expert opinion or when you do not have firsthand knowledge.
4. Have a list of government agencies you (or preferably the buyer) can call to get further information:
    - Give the buyer the proper government departments and numbers to call.
    - Offer to help the buyer but do not volunteer technical information. This information should come directly to the buyer from the government agency.
5. Do not follow a seller's instructions not to disclose defects. The duty to obey a seller's instructions under single agency applies only to lawful instructions.
6. Avoid exaggeration and be conservative with opinions.
7. Recommend that the buyer order a home inspection.
8. Advise the seller to consult an attorney with any questions about the seller's duty to disclose and about how to respond to any question on the property condition disclosure form.

PROGRESS QUIZ

26. When listing a property, what document is MOST helpful in reducing a real estate licensee's liability for misrepresentation claims about property defects?
     a. A radon gas inspection
     b. A lead-based paint inspection
     c. A signed seller's property condition disclosure statement
     d. An appraisal

27. What action(s) will help a residential licensee reduce the risk of lawsuits from the sale of a home?
     a. Refraining from making statements about a property's condition that are not based on firsthand knowledge or expert opinion
     b. Strongly recommending that the buyer order a home inspection
     c. Questioning the seller thoroughly about possible defects to the property
     d. All of the above

LICENSING OF FLORIDA HOME INSPECTORS

Effective July 1, 2010, home inspectors, mold assessors, and mold remediators working in Florida must be licensed. The law requires inspectors to have a high school diploma, be of good character, complete a 120-hour prelicense course, and pass a state exam.

Licenses are effective for up to two years, and licensees must take 14 hours of continuing education before renewing. The law has a "grandfather" clause for persons who meet the requirements of the bill before July 1, 2010. [468.83, F.S.]

Buyers should be encouraged to select their own inspectors; otherwise, buyers may infer collusion between the sales associate and the inspector if the inspector misses one or more important defects. Many excellent home inspectors are members of the American Society of Home Inspectors.

 Web.Link   American Society of Home Inspectors: *www.ashi.org*

The following section is designed to give licensees a better understanding of the work done by a home inspector. It is not a complete description of what the inspector does, but it highlights some important parts of the inspection. Licensees may benefit from knowing how to recognize problems that should be discussed with sellers when listing property or showing property to buyers.

IN PRACTICE

Should You Be Present at the Inspection?

You should try to be present at the property when the home inspector is working to:

- provide support and advice for your customer (either the buyer or the seller), as the process can be intimidating (suggest that your customer withhold any judgments until the inspection report has been delivered);
- ensure that the buyer has an opportunity to ask the inspector questions during the process;
- better understand any issues the inspector finds;
- better understand the inspection process, which will help you explain the process to future buyers and sellers; and
- ensure that if the inspector breaks or damages something that the inspector takes financial responsibility for the problem.

THE NUTS AND BOLTS OF A HOME INSPECTION

One of the most effective risk-management tools available to licensees is a home inspection report prepared for the buyer by a qualified home inspector. When performed properly, the inspection should disclose material defects in a building that buyers, sellers, and real estate licensees might miss. From the licensee's perspective, it is far better that a problem is identified before the closing so the parties can negotiate a settlement. If a material defect is discovered after closing, it is easier for the buyer to sue the licensee than a seller who now lives in a distant city.

INSPECTING THE EXTERIOR

Most home inspectors will start their inspections at the curb in front of the house. The inspector will evaluate the topography of the site. If the ground slopes toward the house or garage, it may result in water seepage. Ground near the perimeter of the house should be graded away from the house so water does not settle in the foundation area. In hilly areas, the water flows may be more of a problem, and water may actually enter the building during periods of heavy rain. The inspector will also note dead trees and limbs and suggest removal of limbs that touch the roof.

Paved Areas

The principal cause of damage to driveways and sidewalks is tree roots. The solution to uneven sections of sidewalk and broken driveway pavement is to cut away the surface roots and repair the paving. Asphalt driveways deteriorate from harsh weather and may need to be patched and resealed to preserve them. Concrete walkways sometimes settle because the base below the sidewalk had been improperly prepared. These problems are not only unsightly, but are also dangerous and should be repaired. If the driveway slopes to the house, the garage and perhaps the house will be exposed to flooding during heavy rain.

The inspector should note cracked or chipped risers in steps leading to the house. The vertical distance between the steps should be equal to prevent a tripping hazard. If there are more than two risers, a rail should be installed. Existing rails must be checked for stability and for rust or rot where they are attached.

Walls

An inspection of the exterior walls includes examining doors and windows. The inspector will generally gauge the uniformity of the wall surface, looking for bulges, cracking, or sagging. Window and door lines should be square. Cracks in masonry at the corners of doors or windows may be evidence of more serious settling problems. Exterior walls of homes in Florida are usually wood-frame or masonry construction. Concrete block and stucco (CBS) was the predominant construction technique in Central and South Florida for many years. In many areas of the state, wood-frame construction is most common.

Siding

If a home has LP siding or synthetic stucco, the licensee should disclose it.

The bottom of the siding should be well above ground level to reduce the chance of rot or termite infestation. Failing composite hardboard lap siding manufactured by Louisiana Pacific (LP siding) and other building materials manufacturers have resulted in class-action lawsuits with decisions in favor of Florida consumers. The siding tends to hold moisture inside and is subject to rot. Synthetic stucco is another problem siding. If not installed correctly, moisture becomes trapped behind the stucco, causing the interior of the wall section to rot.

@ Web.Link

American Siding Consultants: *www.sidingconsultants.com*

Wood siding is subject to deterioration if neglected, requiring expensive repairs. Wherever the siding joins masonry or metal, there is a greater likelihood of water penetration and rot. Unfinished wood siding is subject to mildew and water stains. Painted surfaces are inspected for peeling and weathered areas. Holes should be patched.

Aluminum siding and vinyl siding are both relatively maintenance-free. Aluminum siding should be inspected for dents, but even if there are occasional dents, these are only cosmetic problems and will not affect the durability. Vinyl siding expands during hot weather, and sometimes becomes uneven and wavy.

PROGRESS QUIZ

28. What siding material has had serious problems with wood rot in the siding or framing?
    a. Synthetic stucco
    b. Vinyl siding
    c. Stucco over block
    d. Aluminum siding

Trim

Trim includes the molding around doors and windows, the shutters, the soffit (under roof eaves), and the fascia (edge of the roof eave). Most trim is untreated wood and subject to rot. Trim should be carefully inspected around the edge of the roof, garage doors, and patio sliding doors where rainwater splashes. All exterior trim should be sealed and/or painted to make it watertight

Windows

Jalousie, metal casement, and awning windows are very common in older Florida construction projects. They are opened with window cranks. The cranks should be checked for each window, as they are often inoperable. Energy costs for air-conditioning and heating in houses with these windows are higher because the windows do not close tightly. The single-hung window is becoming the most common window in Florida. Wood casement windows are found in many more expensive homes and are more energy-efficient than the metal casement windows. All windows should be checked for proper operation and good seals from the weather. A careful inspection may show leaks. Thermal-pane windows may be improperly sealed and become cloudy, requiring expensive repairs.

All bedrooms should have at least one operable window with a sill no higher than 42 inches. To allow emergency evacuation, no dimension of the window should be less than 18 inches.

Doors

Some exterior doors have glass areas too close to door locks, making a break-in easier. The inspector will usually recommend that a keyed, dead-bolt lock be installed and the key should be removed when it is not in use. Doors should be checked for rot at the top and bottom and for proper operation. Weather stripping should be recommended.

Decks

Wood columns usually support wood decks. The columns should not touch the soil unless they are pressure-treated. All columns should be checked to ensure that they are firmly attached to the deck. Rotting deck planks should be replaced. Decks more than one foot above the ground should have railings to prevent falls.

Roof

The inspector must examine both the roof covering, such as shingles, and the decking. On pitched roofs, the inspector will check the condition of the covering from the exterior and the decking from the attic. Unevenness and sagging seen from the exterior may be evidence of structural problems, and a professional may be needed to evaluate the condition.

The roof must be adequately vented to stop the roof covering from "cooking" and deteriorating. Ventilation also reduces the moisture that can seep into the decking and cause delamination of the plywood or chipboard. Vent fans with thermostats, as well as passive ridge and soffit vents, are effective. Southern and westerly portions of the roof are likely to have the most heat and deterioration. Curling, pitting, and brittle shingles allow water to penetrate.

Areas around chimneys, vents, and skylights sometimes leak because of poorly installed or deteriorating flashing. The interior inspection should include looking at ceilings and walls under skylights for evidence of leaks.

Garage

If the garage is attached to the house, the doorway leading to the house must be fire-resistant and have a tight seal. Walls and ceilings are inspected for leaks, stains, or patches. The inspector will check to see if the automatic garage door opener works and whether it has an automatic reversing feature to protect children or pets if the door should close on them. The garage door should be checked for proper operation and have a weather seal to prevent water intrusion. The inspector will check for evidence of water stains from water flowing in from the driveway.

Crawlspace

Many homes in Florida are built "above grade," meaning there is a crawlspace under the house. Foundation problems are costly to correct. Basements are relatively rare because Florida's water table is very close to the surface. The inspector is looking for cracks in the foundation walls, termite damage, or rot in wood-support framing and subflooring, sagging joists, and damp ground under the house. The crawlspace should be well ventilated. If air-conditioning ducts are under the floor, the inspector will check for open joints that allow cooled or heated air to escape.

An even larger percentage of houses in Florida are built on slabs and have no crawlspaces. The inspector will check for cracks in the foundation. If the soil was improperly compacted during construction, uneven settling may cause the foundation to crack. A large crack can break plumbing lines and become a serious condition that is expensive to correct.

Wood-Destroying Organisms

Formosan termites have been found in many Florida cities.

Termites are the most important pest problem facing Florida buildings. Nearly one-fourth of all termite damage in the United States occurs in Florida. Only professionals licensed by the state may perform wood-destroying organism (WDO) inspections; most home inspectors are not licensed for preparing WDO reports.

Subterranean termites need dark, damp environments. They must have water and food. The water is generally in the ground and the food is the wood in the building. To have a moist and dark environment in their travels back and forth, they build whitish tubes that are about ¼ inch wide. An inspector can find the tubes in crawlspaces and on outside foundation walls. The walls around hose spigots are likely areas for the tubes. The inspector will break the tube to see if worker termites are traveling within. Termites can find many ways into a building, so the most effective remedy is soil poisoning. They are killed when they enter the soil for water.

Florida homeowners have recently been faced with a much more serious threat: the Formosan termite, one of the most aggressive species of termites in the world. A Formosan colony has millions of termites, is many times the size of native termite colonies, and can devour a pound of wood each day. A story in *Florida Trend* magazine reported that the Formosans have now spread into most of the urban areas of Florida. They have been found in Miami, West Palm Beach, Tampa, Orlando, Tallahassee, and Pensacola. A University of Florida professor stated that the problem is a time bomb for the state and should be treated like a contagious disease. The problem in Louisiana is so serious the state spends more than $300 million annually in its battle to eliminate this feared insect.

Previously, each county in Florida had a different standard for termite prevention for new homes. Requirements in the Florida building code include these standards:

- The sill plate in contact with the concrete slab must be borate-treated wood.
- Generally there should be six inches of clearance between exterior wall coverings that are subject to termite damage and finish grade.

- Roof downspouts and condensate lines shall discharge at least one foot from exterior walls; lawn sprinkler heads must be at least one foot from exterior walls.
- Products for termite protection must be labeled by the state of Florida and the federal government as a preventive treatment for new construction.
- Wooden building components such as decks, fences, and planters shall provide at least 18 inches underneath or six-inch clearances at the top of components to the exterior wall covering or have components easily removable by screws or hinges to allow inspection for termites.

In 2001, a new tropical termite with the scientific name *Nasutitermes costalis* was found in Dania Beach. It looks like an ant and does not respond to chemical baits, but it is not as destructive as the Formosan. This brings the total number of termite species in Florida to 20. One official of the Florida Association of Pest Control Operators says, "Business is good; the bugs are winning."

In 2006, the Florida Department of Agriculture issued new rules for pest control companies:

- Tell consumers if the company did only a spot treatment on a home, and post the information on a treatment sticker on the house. This will alert homebuyers who are told the home has been treated that only a portion of the home was treated, not the entire structure.
- Termite control contracts must state whether the contract covers subterranean termites, drywood termites, or both. If the contract doesn't cover Formosan termites, it must clearly state that fact.
- Companies must re-treat infestations covered by a contract within 90 days (180 days for multiunit buildings). Before 2006, there was no time limit.
- Companies may no longer refuse to re-treat or make repairs if the company knew there was a construction defect (like a water leak) that would encourage infestation and did not notify the owner and give the owner time to correct the problem.

@ **Web.Link**   National Formosan Subterranean Termite Program: *www.ars.usda.gov/is/br/fullstop*

INSPECTING THE INTERIOR

The inspector should check the attic for adequate insulation. Attic ventilation is important, so vent openings should be clear. If the attic is poorly ventilated, the plywood may delaminate. Plumbing vent pipes should not terminate in the attic. Air-conditioning ductwork should be checked to ensure that there are no open joints allowing cooled or heated air to escape. Roof sheathing should be checked for delamination and evidence of leaks. If the inspector notices any sagging during the outside inspection, the framing should be inspected for structural problems.

Air-Conditioning and Heating

The compressor unit should discharge warm air while operating. It should be clean and level, and the airflow area should be clear of obstructions. The condensate drain line should be clear of debris to prevent water backing up and leaking on ceilings or walls. The return air vent should be clear of obstructions.

Heating systems should be checked for age, and maintenance service cards should be attached to heaters. The inspector should check gas or oil heaters for uneven flame patterns that could indicate dangerous defects. Oil burner feed lines should be checked for kinks.

Electrical System

The wires from the electric service pole will be attached to the house at least ten feet above the ground. There will be two or three wires. If only two wires are coming in, the electrical service is probably inadequate. Two wires indicate 110-volt service. Three wires provide the needed 110/220-volt service.

A modern home with central heat and air-conditioning and the normal appliances should have 150- to 200-amp service. The electrical system must be grounded.

Many homes built using aluminum wiring in the late 1960s and early 1970s were later found to be fire hazards. If aluminum wiring was used, the major problems can be corrected by having an electrician replace switches and electrical outlets with those specially designed for the purpose.

Rooms should have one double outlet on each wall. Newer outlets accept three-prong plugs, giving a connection for grounding appliances. Bathroom outlets in newer homes have ground fault circuit breakers to protect against shock. Switches and outlets cannot be accessible from the bathtub or shower for safety reasons.

Plumbing

The water supply system will commonly have a shutoff valve so the water can be turned off for the entire house. The location of the shutoff valve should be shown to the buyer. The inspector will check and operate all fixtures, noting leaks. If water pressure is low, it could indicate some lines blocked from corrosion. Sink and tub drains should open and close properly and be checked for sluggish outflows.

The inspector will inspect water heaters for adequate size and recovery rates for the size of the house. The temperature/pressure relief valve should be installed to flow into a drain line, but it should not spray directly out from the tank where it could endanger anyone nearby.

If there's a septic system, the inspector will check the drain fields for wet spots or lush green grass, signs that the drain fields may be overloaded. Some homeowners with failing septic systems unhook their washing machines and allow them to drain directly outside. This is a code violation and should be noted in the report.

Polybutylene. Polybutylene (PB) is a plastic resin that was used for water supply pipes for about 20 years, starting in 1978. It was cheap, easy to install, and substituted for copper pipe in nearly 25 percent of all homes built during that period. Use of the product typically saved the builder up to $600 per home. The pipes are gray or white with dull finish. PB was also used for underground water mains, which are usually blue, gray, or black.

The problem with the pipes is that they often sprout leaks inside walls or ceilings, requiring extensive repairs and a complete replumbing of the house. The average cost for PB-related repairs is believed to be about $4,000. The problems have been so extensive that the largest class-action lawsuit in history against manufacturers of PB resulted in a $750 million settlement for Texas residents.

The manufacturers of PB, including Shell Oil and DuPont, blame most of the problems on improper installation by plumbers who used plastic or copper fittings to connect to the PB. The manufacturers have addressed the joint problems with new copper crimp fittings that they say fix the leaks.

Homebuyers should ask their home inspector to check the plumbing lines close to the water heaters or in the attic to determine whether they are PB and whether the pipes have the newer copper crimp fittings.

Energy Efficiency

Insulation is measured in R-values.

Caulking and weather stripping are among the most cost-effective steps an owner can take to control energy costs. Actual dollar savings depend on the climate, energy costs, and present efficiency of the house.

Its resistance to heat flow measures insulation effectiveness. Because most areas of Florida experience mild winters, R-values of insulation can be lower than those in northern states. The Department of Energy has established minimum R-values based on zip codes. R-values are additive. If a home has an R-19 insulation in the ceiling and the owner wants to get up to R-30 (recommended), adding more insulation rated at R-11 will achieve the target.

Attic ventilation is important for energy efficiency in Florida homes. If hot air is trapped, excessive heat will not only bake the roof but also make the air conditioner work much harder. Eave vents and gable or ridge vents provide adequate ventilation. Power ventilators are also effective.

PROGRESS QUIZ

29. Which type of plumbing line has been the source of leaks inside walls?
    a. PVC
    b. LP
    c. Polybutylene
    d. EMF

Interior Rooms

Cracked walls and out-of-line doorjambs may be indications of structural problems in rooms. Sometimes the damage may be caused by water leakage. Ceiling discoloration or peeling paint is often evidence of water intrusion.

Bathrooms should have adequate ventilation. Bathrooms with no windows should have operating vent fans. The fan should vent to the outside to avoid excess moisture buildup in the attic. The inspector will check floor areas around the tub and commode for sponginess, an indication of wood rot. Walls around the shower should be checked for firmness. Fixtures should have separate shutoff valves.

ENVIRONMENTAL PROBLEMS

Many contract clauses have been written concerning the environmental problems in or around houses, including radon gas, lead-based paint, asbestos, and electromagnetic fields. Mold has become another major issue for sellers, buyers, and real estate licensees. (See Figure 5.1.)

Radon Gas

While the other environmental concerns mentioned are manmade problems, radon gas is a natural phenomenon. See the discussion of radon gas in chapter 3.

FIGURE 5.1 Environmental Hazards in a Home

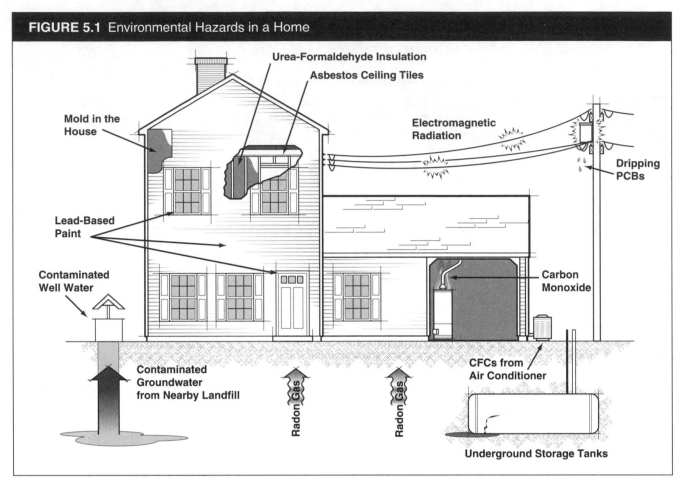

Source: *Modern Real Estate Practice*, 17th Edition, by Galaty, Allaway, and Kyle. Dearborn Real Estate Education Company, Chicago, 2006.

Lead-Based Paint

In 1978, the Consumer Product Safety Commission banned the use of lead-based paint for residential use. Lead-based paint was described in more detail in chapter 3.

Asbestos

Asbestos was installed in many buildings to provide fire retardant and insulation protection. It was also used as backing on vinyl sheet flooring. The mineral fibers in the asbestos become a health hazard when disturbed and may cause cancer and lung scarring. Formerly, asbestos was removed from buildings when it was found. Current practice is to encapsulate it and not disturb it, if possible. If old vinyl flooring is to be removed, an asbestos specialist may be required.

 New

Chinese Drywall

The construction boom of 2004-2007 caused shortages in many building components, including copper, cement, and drywall. One solution to the shortages of drywall was to import large quantities of drywall manufactured in China.

Unfortunately, the manufacturing process was faulty, and the drywall was made of waste from coal-fired plants. Chemicals that seep from the drywall have damaged houses, fixtures, and personal property. Corrosion of copper pipes, wiring, and air-conditioning compressors are serious concerns, while some homeowners complain that the odor makes them ill. While no adverse health effects have been demonstrated, many homeowners are requesting medical monitoring.

More than 10 million square feet was imported into Southwest Florida in 2006 alone. The product is believed to be installed in more than 60,000 homes in 13 states. Currently, a national class action suit is wending its way through the courts and may be one of the largest product liability cases related to home construction in U.S. history.

The drywall looks like any other but smells like rotten eggs. If the words "Knauf" are printed on the back of the drywall (you can check it by going into your attic), you have the Chinese version.

What's to be done? Builders don't yet know whether it will have to be ripped out or whether it can be treated. But it will undoubtedly be very expensive.

Property appraisers, beginning with the 2010 assessment roles, must adjust the assessed value of single-family residential properties affected by tainted drywall. If the home cannot be used for its intended purpose without remediation or repair, the value of the property must be assessed at $0. To qualify, a home must have imported drywall that causes a significant impact on the just value of the property. Also, the buyer must not have been aware of the presence of the tainted drywall at the time of purchase. After substantial completion of remediation and repairs, the property shall be assessed as if the imported drywall had not been present.

IN PRACTICE

Disclose the Presence of Chinese Drywall

If the house was built between 2004 and 2007, there is a possibility that the builder used Chinese drywall. Licensees who list and sell such properties should ensure that full disclosure is made to buyers.

The Florida Association of REALTORS® Form CDA-1, an addendum to the Residential Sale and Purchase Contract:

1. includes a seller's representation that there (is) (is not) Chinese Drywall in the property,
2. gives the buyer an opportunity to have an inspection made and cancel the contract if the defective drywall is found, and
3. states the buyer will hold the broker harmless.

Electromagnetic Radiation

Every day, we are exposed to electromagnetic radiation (EMR), whether it comes from televisions, cell phones, computers, or power lines. Some studies have shown that EMR can cause cancer and leukemia. Wherever there is electric power there is EMR. Because there is a public perception of danger, the presence of high-voltage electric transmission lines may affect the market value of property, requiring disclosure. A concerned buyer may wish to have tests made.

Mold

The hot disclosure term in real estate today is *mold*. Mold is not new; it's been in Florida buildings for years. While the state has not mandated a separate mold disclosure form, many licensees are using the mold disclosure form created by the Florida Association of REALTORS®.

What is mold? Mold is not a plant or animal. It's a type of fungus, and its spores are present in the air we breathe, both indoors and out. We see it on bread or cheese that we keep too long. If we are not good housekeepers, we can see it on the tile grout in the shower. If mold is present in a house, particularly in vacant homes, a "musty" odor is often detected. Mold is often called *mildew*.

The most common indoor molds are *Cladosporium, Penicillium, Aspergillus,* and *Alternaria*. Perhaps the worst type of mold is *Stachybotrys chartarum*, also called *Stachybotrys atra*. It's also called "black mold" because of its greenish-black color, but also could be purple or other colors.

What causes mold in a building? If the spores land in an excessively moist area of our homes, the mold will grow, sometimes very rapidly. Roof leaks, plumbing leaks, condensation, water infiltration, or flooding are common causes of moisture. Wood, drywall, carpeting, and other building materials that become damp can become moldy. Newer materials like pressed wood or particleboard hold moisture for longer periods and are particularly susceptible to mold.

What are the health problems related to mold? Mold is not always a health problem. If a person is sensitive to molds, the symptoms may be nasal stuffiness, eye irritation, or wheezing. More severe reactions can include fever and shortness of breath.

What can be done to prevent the growth of mold in a building? The CDC's recommendations include the following:

- Keep the humidity level in the home below 50 percent
- Use an air conditioner or dehumidifier during the most humid months
- Install exhaust fans in kitchens and bathrooms
- Use mold inhibitors in paint
- Clean the bathroom with mold-killing products
- Do not put carpet in bathrooms
- Remove and replace flooded carpets

What can be done to reduce the levels of mold in a building? Because mold spores are everywhere, mold cannot be totally eliminated. But once mold has been found, the following steps can be taken to kill *Stachybotrys chartarum*:

- Find out what is causing the moisture and eliminate it
- Clean mold off surfaces with a weak bleach solution
- Carpets with mold underneath should be removed
- Moldy wallboard and insulation should be replaced
- In flood-damaged areas, clean with water and chlorine bleach (10-to-1 ratio)

@ Web.Link Environmental Protection Agency Web site on mold: *www.epa.gov/mold/moldresources.html*

PROGRESS QUIZ

30. Which type of household mold, sometimes called "black mold," seems to cause most health problems?
    a. Cladosporium
    b. Aspergillus
    c. Alternaria
    d. Stachybotrys atra

Case Study

AIR CONDITIONER INSPECTION REPORT CHANGED BY LICENSEE

- **Facts:** A married couple submitted an offer to purchase a house with a contingency clause requiring that a home inspection show no substantive defects. The couple was represented by Sales Associate Nancy. The respondent, Sales Associate Margaret, represented the sellers. The home inspection report later showed that the "air-conditioning does not appear to be cooling enough."

Nancy contacted an air-conditioning contractor to make an inspection, and she met the technician at the property. The technician said the unit was low on Freon, but the biggest problem was the age of the unit (13 years old). Sales Associate Nancy authorized him to install the Freon and give her a copy of the work order showing it had been done. He gave her the pink copy of the work order that also showed his recommendation that the unit be replaced. According to Sales Associate Margaret, Nancy called and told her about the Freon, but not that the unit should be replaced. She also said the buyers "were OK with it."

Respondent Margaret did not see the repairman's report until just before closing and was upset by the recommendation for replacement. She tried to contact the repairman for more information but was unsuccessful. She later claimed she told Nancy that if she didn't hear back from him soon, she was going to remove the recommendation from the work order. Sales Associate Nancy disputes this.

Thereafter, Margaret gave the buyers an altered copy of the repairman's report, with the recommendation for replacement deleted. The transaction was closed, and the buyers occupied the property. A month later, the unit failed, costing $2,300 to replace. When the buyers investigated further, Margaret told them she felt that because the repairman wouldn't return her calls, she had the right as a licensee to alter the report.

- **Questions:**

1. Did Sales Associate Margaret violate the law?

2. What sections of Chapter 475, F.S., did Margaret violate?

3. What should Sales Associate Margaret's punishment be?

- **Determination of Violation:** The administrative law judge (ALJ) found Margaret had violated Section 475.(1), F.S., to wit: attempted concealment and breach of trust.

- **Penalty:** The Florida Real Estate Commission entered a Final Order suspending Margaret's real estate license for six months and fined her $1,000.

Chapter 6

Fair Housing and the Americans with Disabilities Act

In This Chapter

Civil Rights Acts of 1866 and 1968 ● Who is covered by the act? ● Florida Fair Housing Act ● Local fair housing acts ● Americans with Disabilities Act ● Florida Americans with Disabilities Act ● AIDS patients and housing

Learning Objectives

When you have completed this chapter, you should be able to:

● list the categories of persons protected under the Fair Housing Act,

● list at least five discriminatory practices prohibited by the Fair Housing Act,

● describe the exception to "adults only" prohibitions,

● state which HUD form must be posted in all real estate offices,

● describe at least four requirements of the Florida Americans with Disabilities Act, and

● answer each question on the fair housing case study.

CIVIL RIGHTS ACTS OF 1866 AND 1968

The Civil Rights Act of 1866 was passed just after the Civil War to prohibit discrimination based on race. For many years, the law was not widely enforced, but in 1968, the U.S. Supreme Court upheld the law in *Jones v. Mayer*. Subsequent court actions requiring compliance with the law have been numerous and successful.

The Civil Rights Act of 1968 included Title VIII, "The Fair Housing Act." The act has been amended several times to protect against discrimination in housing, and it now covers race, color, religion, sex, national origin, handicap, or familial status (presence of children or pregnant women).

IN PRACTICE

Protect Yourself and Your Customers by Knowing the Law

Your license, self-esteem, and your wallet depend on your following every requirement of the law. It won't help to say that you didn't know you couldn't do that or that you were only trying to help.

Be sure to discuss the law with your buyers and sellers, showing them language in the contract. Get your seller's written consent to abide by the law, and walk away from the listing if you become aware of illegal discrimination.

Be certain to treat every buyer with equal service; don't require one person to be preapproved before you show a house if you don't have that policy for everyone.

Race and Color

Real estate advertisements should not indicate the racial makeup of a neighborhood. An ad that said "Excellent area with many Asian families" would be a clear violation. Sales associates may never steer buying prospects into a neighborhood based on the buyer's description of racial or ethnic characteristics.

Religion

Licensees should not advertise that a home is near St. Thomas Catholic Church or that the neighborhood is within walking distance to Temple Israel Day School. A broker's ad that says "Looking for good Christian family to rent one side of duplex" violates the law.

Sex

Advertisements for single-family dwellings or apartments may not describe a preference or limitation based on sex. "Single female roommate wanted" is allowed as an exception for shared-living advertising.

National Origin

Steering a Cuban family into a neighborhood because they want to live in a Spanish-speaking area is a violation. Advertising for "English-speaking tenant only" is a limitation and is illegal.

Handicap

Licensees who advertise "not wheelchair accessible" violate the law. However, it is acceptable to advertise that a residence is "handicapped accessible" or that it has a "wheelchair ramp for accessibility."

Familial Status

Families with children or pregnant women are protected under the law. Advertisements that limit the number or ages of children violate the law.

WHO IS COVERED BY THE ACT?

The law applies to persons who own four or more homes; multifamily properties (except properties with fewer than four units, one of which is occupied by the owner); residential property when the owner, during the immediate past two-year period, sells two or more houses in which the owner was not a resident; and transactions in which a broker is involved. While it appears that a private owner may discriminate under the 1968 Act, under certain circumstances, the 1866 Act clearly prohibits racial discrimination.

The following actions by covered owners or brokers are specifically prohibited if they discriminate against a protected person (see Figure 6.1 for examples):

- *Steering* in real estate ads or in showing properties by guiding homebuyers into a neighborhood
- *Blockbusting* a neighborhood by attempting to frighten a homeowner into selling
- *Redlining* by lenders who have different conditions and terms for loans made in certain areas
- Refusing to rent to, sell to, or negotiate with a party
- Quoting different terms or conditions for buying or renting
- Making a false statement about the availability of housing
- Denying membership in any real estate service
- Making discriminatory statements about the availability of housing

One of the most common violations involves steering. Some licensees who never intended to discriminate are guilty of steering, but at the end of the day the result is the same regardless of intent. For example, if a buyer is shown homes in neighborhoods that are predominantly the same as the buyer's protected class when other, more diverse neighborhoods have homes that are available, that could be construed as discrimination.

IN PRACTICE

Are You Unintentionally Violating the Law?

To avoid a charge of discrimination, monitor yourself. Ask yourself as you set up the list of homes to show, "Would I show the same homes if my prospective buyers were of a different race?" If the answer is "No," you have cause for concern. If a buyer selects the neighborhoods by name, no problem. If you suggest neighborhoods, be sure you are not adding or deleting areas based on racial or ethnic bias.

PROGRESS QUIZ

31. If a broker complies with an owner's instructions to restrict prospective tenants to Christian persons, will the broker violate the Fair Housing Act?
    a. Yes, because it shows a preference or limitation based on religion.
    b. No, because single homeowners are not exempt from the act.
    c. No, single homeowners are exempt from the act when using a broker.
    d. No, because religious preference is not a legal violation.

Licensees should not advertise properties in a minority area in publications aimed at specific minority groups, unless the licensee advertises nonminority properties in the same publication.

IN PRACTICE

Don't Engage in Discriminatory Behavior with a Buyer

If a buyer asks you about the ethnic characteristics of a neighborhood, don't get involved in the conversation. This response is likely to keep you out of trouble:

"I appreciate having the opportunity to work with you in finding a home. The law and our company's policy do not allow me to show you homes based on the racial, religious, or ethnic characteristics of a neighborhood. So, I won't be able to place any such restrictions on showings or information about the availability of homes for sale or for rent."

"Adults Only" Designations

"Adults only" designations are prohibited by the familial status provision, with one exception: communities with the status of "housing for older persons." Requirements for such a community are as follows (either number 1 or number 2, not both):

1. The housing must be specifically designed and operated to assist elderly persons and is intended for, and solely occupied by, persons 62 years of age or older, or
2. The housing is intended and operated for occupancy by persons 55 years of age or older who meet these requirements:
   - At least 80 percent of the occupied units are occupied by at least one person 55 years of age or older.
   - The facility or community publishes and adheres to policies and procedures that demonstrate its intent to in fact be a provider of housing for older persons.
   - The facility or community complies with rules established by HUD for verification of occupancy.

Communities with housing for older persons should register with the Florida Commission on Human Relations, but failure to register does not jeopardize the community's legal status.

For more information, see the Commission's Web site at: *http://fchr.state.fl.us/55_communities_1*

Other Requirements

Managers of apartment properties may not assign families with children or any other protected class to segregated areas. Owners may set reasonable rules for maximum occupancy in apartment buildings. Owners and licensees should obtain legal advice before establishing such rules.

Brokers must post the Fair Housing Poster in all offices. Failure to do so shifts the burden of proof in discrimination actions to the broker. It is the broker's responsibility to provide training and supervision to ensure compliance with the law. A poster is included in the Forms-To-Go section.

Complaint Process

To report violations of the Fair Housing Act, contact:

Office of Fair Housing and Equal Opportunity, U.S. Department of Housing and Urban Development (HUD), Room 5204, Washington, DC 20410-2000

Toll-free hotline: 800-669-9777
TDD: 800-927-9275

Persons have one year to file a complaint with the U.S. Department of Housing and Urban Development (HUD). The complaint should include:

- the complainant's name and address,
- the name and address of the person or company that is the subject of the complaint,
- the address or other identification of the housing involved,
- a short description of the facts that caused the complainant to believe rights were violated, and
- the dates of the alleged violation.

HUD will notify the complaining party when it receives the complaint. Normally, HUD also will:

- notify the alleged violator of the complaint and permit the person to submit an answer,
- investigate the complaint and determine whether there is a reasonable cause to believe the Fair Housing Act has been violated, and
- notify the complainant if it cannot complete an investigation within 100 days of receiving the complaint.

@ **Web.Link**

National Fair Housing Advocate Online: *www.fairhousing.com*

HUD Office of Fair Housing and Equal Opportunity: *www.hud.gov/offices/fheo*

U.S. Department of Housing and Urban Development—Fair Housing Laws: *www.hud.gov/offices/fheo/FHLaws/index.cfm*

PROGRESS QUIZ

32. A licensee is the single agent for a minority couple. He says, "Are you more comfortable buying a home in a neighborhood with people of your race?" Does this question violate any laws?
    a. Yes, this is an illegal act called *blockbusting*.
    b. Yes, this is an illegal question that is considered *steering*.
    c. No, if he is a single agent, he needs to know their housing needs.
    d. No, as long as the agent does not decide which neighborhood to show.

FLORIDA FAIR HOUSING ACT (CHAPTER 760, F.S.)

The Florida Fair Housing Act is modeled after the federal Fair Housing Act and prohibits discrimination based on race, color, religion, sex, national origin, familial status, or handicap. The principal reason that Florida has its own fair housing law is that suing in a state court gives victims of discrimination another, perhaps easier, remedy than trying to bring a federal case.

Discrimination in the Sale or Rental of Housing

Chapter 760.23, F.S., prohibits discrimination against a person protected under this section in the sale or rental of housing. Specifically, the following actions are unlawful:

- To refuse to sell or rent, to refuse to negotiate for the sale or rental of, or otherwise to make unavailable or deny a dwelling
- To discriminate against any person in the terms, conditions, or privileges of sale or rental of a dwelling, or in the provision of services or facilities in connection therewith
- To publish any notice, statement, or advertisement with respect to the sale or rental of a dwelling that indicates any preference, limitation, or discrimination
- To represent that any dwelling is not available for inspection, sale, or rental when such dwelling is in fact so available
- To induce or attempt to induce, for profit, any person to sell or rent any dwelling by a representation regarding the entry into the neighborhood of a person or persons of a particular race, color, national origin, sex, handicap, familial status, or religion

LOCAL FAIR HOUSING ACTS

Many cities and counties in Florida have passed local fair housing acts. These acts mirror the federal Fair Housing Act but cover classes that are not included in the federal or state housing acts, such as age, marital status, and sexual orientation. Licensees must be aware of the requirements of these acts to ensure that they are in compliance.

FIGURE 6.1 Fair Housing Act Restrictions

Prohibited Action	Example of Violation
Refusing to sell, rent, or negotiate the sale or rental of housing	John is the property manager of an apartment building with 125 units. When a minority family asks to look at some of the apartments, he tells them to go away.
Changing the terms or conditions or services for different individuals as a method of screening	Linda is the owner of a 20-unit apartment building. She is very religious, and when a non-Christian family asks to look at a $300 apartment, she tells them that the $300 price is a discount for Christians and their rent would be $340.
Advertising any discriminatory preference or limitation in housing or making any inquiry or reference that is discriminatory in nature	Broker Bill places the following advertisement in the *Miami Herald:* "Just listed! Beautiful 3-bedroom home with Spanish barrel-tile roof. Perfect for Cuban families!" Developer Jean has an ad that says: "Be a happy homeowner in Bellair Gardens." The ad has a photo of several African-American families.
Falsely representing that a property is not for sale	Mildred, a person with disabilities, looks at a single-family home and is told that the home is no longer available. The next day, Mildred sees the home advertised and a "for rent" sign in front of the house.
Profiting by inducing property owners to sell or rent based on the prospective entry into the neighborhood of persons of a protected class	Sales Associate Josie sends a newsletter to homeowners in a predominantly white neighborhood. The newsletter features Josie's real estate achievements and a request to call her to list property. On the cover of the newsletter is a photo showing several racial minorities. The title of the newsletter is "The Changing Face of Sunland Station."
Altering the terms or conditions of a home loan or denying a loan, as a means of discrimination	A lender requires that Mary, a divorced mother of three children, pay for a credit report and have her father cosign her application. A male friend who worked with her and had lower income than she did and also poor credit told her that he was not required to do either of those things.
Denying membership or participation in a multiple listing service, a real estate organization, or another facility related to the sale or rental of housing as a means of discrimination	The Orange County Realty Council meets weekly to market available properties. The Council has restricted membership to Caucasian males, rejecting applications from women and African Americans.

Adapted from *Modern Real Estate Practice*, 17th Edition, by Galaty, Allaway, and Kyle. Dearborn Real Estate Education, Chicago, 2006.

AMERICANS WITH DISABILITIES ACT (ADA)

The ADA prohibits discrimination based on disability in employment, programs, and services provided by state and local governments, as well as goods and services provided by private companies and commercial facilities. A disability is defined by the ADA as a physical or mental impairment that substantially limits a major life activity, such as walking, seeing, hearing, learning, breathing, caring for oneself, or working. The Department of Justice administers the law.

The ADA does not cover temporary impairments such as broken bones or sexual or behavioral disorders. Homosexuality, which is not a disability, is not covered under the law, nor are persons who are currently abusing drugs or alcohol.

Full compliance with the ADA is required for new construction and alteration. Existing structures must be made accessible when that goal is readily achievable, meaning that the goal can be carried out without great difficulty or expense. The factors for determining whether changes are readily achievable are described in more detail in the ADA regulations issued by the Department of Justice, and the ADA regulations should be consulted for more detail. A tax deduction of up to $15,000 is available for removing barriers at existing places of business.

Parking Areas

Parking areas should have one accessible space for every 25 total regular parking spaces. The accessible parking space should be eight feet wide for a car, with a five-foot access aisle. At least one space must be van accessible (eight feet wide with an eight-foot access aisle, and at least 98 inches of vertical clearance). The accessible spaces should be the closest available to the accessible entrance.

Access to Buildings

People with disabilities should be able to approach a building and enter as freely as everyone else. Curbs at the entrance should have curb cuts. The route of travel should be at least 36 inches wide, stable, and slip-resistant. An object must be within 27 inches of the ground in order to be detected by a person using a cane. Overhead objects must be higher than 80 inches for headroom.

Ramps

For every inch of height, ramps should have at least one foot of length (1:12) and have a railing at least 34 inches high. There must be a five-foot-long level landing at every 30-foot horizontal length of ramp, at the top and bottom of the ramp, and at switchbacks.

Entrances

Inaccessible entrances should have signs showing the closest accessible entrance. A service entrance should not be used as the accessible entrance unless there are no other options. Entrance doors should have at least 32 inches of clear opening, with at least 18 inches of clear wall space on the pull side of the door. Door handles should be no higher than 48 inches and operable with a closed fist. Doors in public areas should have openings of at least 32 inches.

Aisles and Pathways

Aisles and pathways to services should be at least 36 inches wide. Spaces in auditoriums should be distributed throughout the hall. Tops of tables or counters should be between 28 and 34 inches high.

Restrooms

Restrooms should be accessible to people with disabilities. If a restroom is inaccessible, there should be a sign giving directions to an accessible restroom. A wheelchair-accessible stall that is at least five feet square is necessary to make turns. Grab bars should be behind and on the sidewall nearest the toilet. At least one lavatory should have a 30-inch-wide by 48-inch-deep clear space in front. The bottom of the lavatory should be no lower than 29 inches; the rim should be no higher than 34 inches. The faucets should be operable with one closed fist.

The ADA requires that state and local governments provide access to programs offered to the public. The ADA also covers effective communication with people with disabilities and eligibility criteria that may restrict or prevent access, and it requires reasonable modifications of policies and practices that may be discriminatory.

 Web.Link   U.S. Department of Justice: ADA home page: *www.ada.gov*

FLORIDA AMERICANS WITH DISABILITIES ACT (CHAPTER 760, F.S.)

The Florida Americans with Disabilities Act implements and mirrors portions of the Americans with Disabilities Act and includes other important provisions. Florida has its own act because suing in a state court gives victims of discrimination another remedy for violations.

It is unlawful to discriminate against any person in the terms, conditions, or privileges of residential sales or rentals because a buyer, renter, or one of their associates has a disability. Owners and managers must permit, at the expense of the handicapped person, reasonable modifications of existing premises to be occupied by such person if such modifications may be necessary to afford such person full enjoyment of the premises. Owners and managers may not refuse to make reasonable accommodations in rules, policies, practices, or services, when such accommodations may be necessary to afford people with disabilities an equal opportunity to use and enjoy a dwelling.

New multifamily dwellings must be designed and constructed to have at least one building entrance on an accessible route, unless doing so is impractical because of the terrain. All doors designed to allow passage into and within such dwellings must be wide enough to allow passage by a person in a wheelchair. Light switches, electrical outlets, thermostats, and other environmental controls must be in accessible locations. Reinforcements must be installed in bathroom walls to allow later installation of grab bars. Kitchens and bathrooms must be built so that a person in a wheelchair can easily maneuver in the spaces.

PROGRESS QUIZ

33. Broker Gilda manages a single-family home for the Smiths. Harry, a person with disabilities, wants to rent the property and wants to make alterations, including a ramp at the entrance, lowering the kitchen counters, and widening some of the doorways. He agrees to pay for the remodeling and for restoring the premises at the end of the lease term. Which is correct?

    a. Owners of single-family homes are not required to comply with the Americans with Disabilities Act.

    b. Broker Gilda should suggest that Harry find another home that has already been remodeled for people with disabilities.

    c. The owners could refuse to allow the alterations, but must do so by stating that the renovations are "not readily achievable."

    d. If Gilda explains that the owners will not allow the alterations, she would violate the law.

All new residential construction must have at least one bathroom that is "accessible" as defined by law. Any new or renovated building frequented by the public must comply in the areas of landings, curb ramps, low-pull-force doors, seating spaces, aisles, and public restrooms.

PROGRESS QUIZ

34. The vertical height for a wheelchair-accessible ramp is 30 inches. How many feet must the ramp be to meet the ADA guidelines?

    a. 12

    b. 16

    c. 24

    d. 30

AIDS PATIENTS AND HOUSING (CHAPTERS 689.25 AND 760.50, F.S.)

The fact that an occupant of real property is infected with human immunodeficiency virus (HIV) or diagnosed with acquired immune deficiency syndrome (AIDS) is not a material fact that must be revealed in a real estate transaction. An owner of real property or the owner's agent may not be sued for the failure to disclose to the buyer or tenant that an occupant of the property was infected with HIV or AIDS. [689.25, F.S.]

Such disclosure also would violate the law that prohibits discrimination against people who have AIDS and an HIV infection. Any person with or perceived as having AIDS or HIV is entitled to every protection available to people with disabilities, including fair housing protections. [760.50, F.S.]

PROGRESS QUIZ

35. Mary is showing her listing to William. John, the owner of the property, has been diagnosed with AIDS. What should Mary do with respect to disclosure?

   a. Mary should not volunteer the information, but if asked, is permitted to disclose the information.

   b. Mary has the duty to make disclosure because the information may materially affect the value of the property.

   c. Disclosure of the fact would be a violation of the law.

   d. Mary must ask John when taking the listing if it is all right to disclose the information to prospective buyers.

Case Study

AN OWNER DISCRIMINATES BASED ON RACE

● **Facts:** The complainant, a black man, saw a house with a For Rent sign. He asked the two women on the porch if the house was still for rent. The older white female introduced herself as the owner and said it was not yet rented, but the lady she was with had first choice. The complainant left.

Later the complainant spoke to his supervisor at work, a white female, who offered to call the respondent. First the complainant called, got her voice mail, and left a message. His supervisor called immediately afterward and started to leave a message, but was interrupted when the respondent answered the phone. The complainant's supervisor told the respondent she was inquiring about the rental for a friend.

The respondent asked, "What color is he, black or white?" The supervisor responded that it was illegal to ask such a question. The respondent stated that she did not want a black person renting the house as it was in a predominantly white neighborhood and she did not want the neighbors damaging her house.

Finally, the respondent agreed to talk with the complainant by phone, and the supervisor listened in on an extension. The respondent then asked a long series of questions, including who the complainant intended to vote for in the upcoming presidential election. After many requests, the respondent agreed to show the property the next day at 5 PM.

The complainant met the respondent, who said she required a down payment that included the application fee in cash, but refused to give a receipt. The complainant said he needed a receipt, but the respondent said he would have to have more trust. The respondent also stated that she would need $35 for and extensive background check and could find out information that "only the FBI would have."

● **Questions:**

1. Did the respondent refuse to negotiate for the rental of, or otherwise make unavailable, a dwelling to any person because of race?

_____

_____

_____

2. What penalty should be assessed against the respondent?

_____

_____

_____

● **Determination of Violation:** The administrative law judge found that the respondent had violated the Fair Housing Act, discriminating based on race.

● **Penalty:** The administrative law judge awarded the complainant damages including compensation for damages sustained and for emotional distress, embarrassment, humiliation, inconvenience, and the loss of housing opportunity. The ALJ and also awarded a civil penalty in the amount of $11,000 against the respondent.

Chapter

7

Real Estate Finance— Laws and Trends

In This Chapter

Housing and mortgage crisis ● Mortgage fraud ● Home Valuation Code of Conduct ● The Real Estate Settlement Procedures Act ● Truth-in-Lending ● The Equal Credit Opportunity Act ● Fair credit reporting ● Homeowners Protection Act of 1998 ● HUD's predatory lending rule restricts "flipping" ● Other trends in financing real property ● Short sales

Your Quick Reference Guide to the Major Changes in Finance

Important changes you should carefully review:

● New FHA appraisal requirements

● Changes to Florida's Appraisal Law

● New RESPA requirements change Good Faith Estimate and HUD-1 Settlement Statement

● Brand new regulation for Florida mortgage brokers

● FHASecure helps owners save their homes.

Learning Objectives

When you have completed this chapter, you should be able to:

● describe at least three factors that contributed to the housing crisis,

● list five types of mortgage fraud,

● list the types of information in a real estate advertisement that will trigger the need for Truth-in-Lending disclosures,

● list the categories of protected parties under the Equal Credit Opportunity Act,

● describe the types of income that a lender must consider when evaluating a loan application,

- describe the applicant's rights if a loan application is rejected,
- give the two most important reasons that decisions on loan applications can be made almost immediately,
- list at least five types of information used in a credit-scoring system, and
- describe the basic steps used in a short sale.

HOUSING AND MORTGAGE CRISIS

During the years 2003–2006, the United States experienced the biggest housing boom in its history, a boom that began to deflate in 2007, causing a meltdown in the credit markets. The fault belongs everywhere in the system, but perhaps the great engine of the catastrophe was Wall Street. Large banks, hedge funds, and investment firms had losses of a magnitude never imagined, eroding their capital bases and requiring large infusions of capital to avoid a systemic failure. The Federal Reserve worked to hold the system together to prevent catastrophic failure of the credit system.

In September 2008, Fannie Mae and Freddie Mac were placed under the conservatorship of the Federal Housing Finance Agency, one of the most sweeping government interventions in private financial markets in many years.

Some of the causes for this event include the following:

- Speculation by investors who put deposits on two, five, or ten preconstruction units that they expected to sell before they had to close. This resulted in a huge increase in the construction of new homes and condominiums that were not built based on a need for shelter, but based on the desire to make money by flipping the contracts. When the market slowed, the speculators walked away from their (usually small) deposits, leaving the builders with huge inventories of unsold homes.
- Mortgage fraud situations perpetrated by mortgage brokers, lenders, appraisers, title insurance personnel, real estate brokers, buyers, and sellers. Mortgage fraud is discussed more thoroughly in the following section.
- People bought homes they could not afford because lenders made it easy. Many lenders made loans where the housing expense ratio was at 60 percent—meaning the house payment for a person making $5,000 monthly would pay $3,000 in mortgage payments. That was substantially higher that the FHA guideline of 31 percent (which says the individual should have payments no higher than $1,550).
- Special-purpose vehicles (SPVs) allowed loans to be bundled into large securities backed by mortgage payments. In 2006, mortgage origination volume surged to $2.5 trillion. Investors didn't know much about subprime loans, and they could never have been sold, except for bond rating agencies like Moodys, Standard and Poor, and Fitch, who put the gold seal on the securities. Moodys's profits surged. When the bonds later soured, Moodys downgraded those securities, but it was too late for the investors. Later, collateralized debt obligations (CDOs) were set up that purchased SPVs then sold bonds to investors. These bonds didn't have real mortgages to back them up; they were one step removed, so the trouble was compounded.
- Banks, brokerage firms, and hedge funds found the securitization of mortgages very profitable, selling "tranches," which are parts of a package ("tranche" is a French word meaning "slice"). The bond tranches have different risks,

rewards, and/or maturities. It's similar to betting on a football game. The basic bet is who wins; however, another bet could be the point spread, another the number of touchdown passes thrown by a given quarterback, and so on. A typical security would have 10 or 12 classes of bonds, rated from triple-A to much lower grades. The highest-rated bond buyers, having lower risk, would accept a lower interest rate. The low-rated bonds, much riskier, would pay a higher rate, but those buyers would take the first loss. Many of these banks and investment firms had contracts with large mortgage companies to originate mortgages; for example, one contract required New Century Mortgage (now defunct) to originate and package $2 billion in loans each month. When the pressure is on to produce that kind of volume, one should expect that the quality of the loans will be lower than expected.

- Because of the credit and liquidity problems, lenders are more cautious and private mortgage insurance companies are in financial trouble, so even qualified buyers find it more difficult to get financing for their purchases, further exacerbating the problem.

The price increases fueled by the rampant speculation almost certainly will have to be given back. If one takes the annual median family income of Americans over the years from 1980 to 2000 and divides it into the median home price, the multiplier was about 2.5. That could be considered the norm. Looking at that statistic in 2008, the median home price divided by the median family income is at about 4.07, compared to 5.1 in 2007. The implications are serious because median income is quite stable. If the ratio comes back to the norm, it would require prices to deflate very significantly over the coming years.

It will take many years to work out the mess. Investors lost billions, people lost their homes, jobs were lost, and even homeowners who were not involved have lost the character of their neighborhoods because of foreclosed, shuttered homes.

Lenders, Congress, the administration, and scholars have a lot to evaluate in making proposals to keep the system going, helping homeowners who are dealing with foreclosure, and establishing regulations to prevent a future financial crisis.

MORTGAGE FRAUD

The FBI has made mortgage fraud one of its top priorities because of the huge volume of losses to banks and investors. Figure 7.1 shows the shocking trends.

Mortgage brokers, appraisers, real estate licensees, sellers, buyers, builders, and others have been found guilty of financial fraud, identity theft, mail fraud, and other charges, carrying sentences of up to 30 years in prison. All fraudulent flipping and nearly all other organized fraud schemes that were reviewed relied on fraudulent appraisals.

FBI fraud cases include the following:

- **Property flipping**—Property is purchased, improperly appraised at a higher value, then quickly sold. This practice involves fraudulent appraisals, doctored loan documentation, inflated buyer income, etc.
- **Silent second mortgage**—The buyer borrows the down payment from a seller through the issuance of an undisclosed second mortgage. The lender on the first mortgage thinks the buyer has invested his own money in a down payment, when in fact the funds are borrowed. This is also done sometimes by builders who have a large inventory of unsold homes. In other cases, a buyer agrees to pay a much-inflated price for property, with the difference in the inflated value and the fair value of the home in a "disappearing second" held

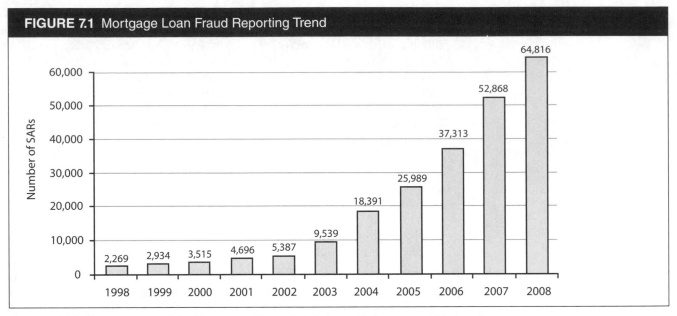

FIGURE 7.1 Mortgage Loan Fraud Reporting Trend

Source: U.S. Department of the Treasury, Financial Crimes Enforcement Network.

by the mortgage broker. After the closing, the mortgage broker tears up the second mortgage papers, then sells the loan as a 75 percent loan-to-value ("safer") loan when the borrower truly paid nothing down.

- **Nominee loans**—The identity of the borrower is concealed through the use of a nominee (also called a straw buyer) who allows the borrower to use the nominee's name and credit history to apply for the loan.
- **Stolen identity**—The applicant's name, personal identifying information, and credit history are used without the true person's knowledge.
- **Equity skimming**—An investor may use a straw buyer, false income documents, or false credit reports to obtain a mortgage in the straw buyer's name. After closing, the straw buyer signs over the property with a quitclaim deed to an investor. The investor rents the property without making payments on the mortgage until foreclosure takes place several months later.
- **Air loans**—This loan is totally false. The mortgage broker invents a property and a borrower. The broker sets up a bank of telephones for verifications and poses as the employer, another as the appraiser, another as the credit agency, etc.
- **Chunking**—A swindler holds a seminar promising to show investors how to get rich buying property with no money down. Using the investors' personal information, the swindler submits multiple mortgage applications, pocketing the loan proceeds.

The FBI has compiled this list of activities that it believes could indicate mortgage fraud:

- **Inflated appraisals,** usually involving the exclusive use of one appraiser
- **Higher than customary commissions and fees** paid to brokers and appraisers
- **Falsification of loan applications,** with mortgage brokers showing buyers how to falsify the application, or asking a borrower to sign a blank application
- **Fake supporting loan documentation,** with buyers being asked to sign blank employee or bank forms
- **Purchase loans disguised as refinance,** typically requiring less documentation by the lender

To protect from becoming a victim of mortgage fraud, consumers should do the following:

- **Get referrals** for real estate and mortgage professionals. Check the licenses of the industry professionals with state, county, or city regulatory agencies.
- **Know that if it sounds too good to be true, it probably is.** An outrageous promise of extraordinary profit in a short period of time signals a problem.
- **Be wary of strangers and unsolicited contacts,** as well as high-pressure sales techniques.
- **Look at written information** to include recent comparable sales in the area and other documents such as tax assessments to verify the value of the property.
- **Understand what they are signing and agreeing to.** If they do not understand, they should reread the documents or seek assistance from an attorney.
- **Make sure the name on the application matches** the name on your identification.
- **Review the title history** to determine if the property has been sold multiple times within a short period—it could mean that this property has been "flipped" and the value falsely inflated.
- **Know and understand the terms of the mortgage.** Check the information against the information in the loan documents to ensure they are accurate and complete.
- **Never sign any loan documents that contain blanks,** which leaves consumers vulnerable to fraud.

Florida's Response to Mortgage Fraud

Florida is stepping up its enforcement efforts with changes to Section 494, F.S., effective October 1, 2007. These changes provide that a person (including a real estate licensee) commits fraud by knowingly lying, misrepresenting, or omitting material information that the lender or another party in the transaction would rely on in the mortgage lending process. Additionally, the changes provide for the following:

- Mortgage brokers and lenders must give borrowers detailed disclosures for loans, including adjustable-rate mortgages (ARMs).
- The mortgage broker must give borrowers written disclosure about how much a lender is paying the mortgage broker.
- Good-faith estimates must be signed and dated by the borrower, and it must disclose the "recipient of all fees charged." The law allows the fees to be disclosed in generic terms.
- Borrowers must be notified in writing no later than three business days before closing if any of the loan terms have changed. The mortgage broker must be able to prove that the notice was provided and that the borrower accepted the new terms.
- The Florida Office of Financial Regulation will discipline mortgage brokers and mortgage lenders who violate the Real Estate Settlement Procedures Act (RESPA) or the federal Truth-in-Lending Act.

As a result of the housing and financial crisis, Chapter 494 was changed in many areas to better protect Florida's consumers.

Effective January 1, 2010 Persons who engage in loan modification activities must be licensed under Chapter 494.

Loan originators working as employees of lenders are no longer exempt from licensing. Loan modification activities require the borrower's written consent. The modifier may charge fees only after performing all services under the agreement, and only if the modification results in material benefit to the borrower.

Effective September 1, 2010 All mortgage broker, mortgage brokerage business, correspondent mortgage lender, and mortgage lender licenses issued before October 1, 2010 expired on December 31, 2010. Persons with an active mortgage broker license issued before October 1, 2010 who applied for the new loan originator license between October 1, 2010 and December 31, 2010 may continue to operate until the Office of Financial Regulation either approves or denies the loan originator license. The Office shall have 60 days to issue a deficiency letter and 180 days to approve or deny a completed application.

Effective October 1, 2010 Applicants and licensees must submit filings on uniform forms via the Nationwide Mortgage Licensing System and Registry (NMLS). The application review will include not only a criminal background check, but a review of the applicant's credit history. Applicants who have a bankruptcy, or who have chargeoffs must provide a satisfactory explanation.

License titles were changed as follows: Individual Mortgage Broker to Loan Originator and Mortgage Brokerage Business to Mortgage Broker. Mortgage Lender license is unchanged. The following license titles were repealed: Mortgage Business Schools, Correspondent Mortgage Lenders, and Savings Clause Mortgage Lenders.

The law established a Mortgage Broker Guaranty Trust Fund, somewhat like the Real Estate Recovery Fund, with payments into the fund by applicants and licensees. Payment from the fund in settlement of a claim against a licensee will result in revocation of the license.

All licenses issued under Chapter 494 shall be renewed annually by December 31 via the NMLS. A criminal background check and a credit report are required for each renewal.

The principal loan originator or branch manager must sign and date the mortgage broker agreement, and include the loan originator's unique NMLS identifier. Fees received by the business (mortgage broker) from a borrower must be identified as a loan origination fee, with the exception of application and third-party fees. Fees must be disclosed in dollar amounts.

The Office may summarily suspend a license if there is reason to believe that a licensee poses an immediate, serious danger to the public's health, safety, or welfare, if the licensee has been arrested for any felony crime or any crime involving fraud, dishonesty, breach of trust, money laundering, or any other act of moral turpitude.

Mortgage lenders must meet specific net worth requirements depending on the activities of the lender and provide financial statements to the Office.

The law added penalties for:

1. Attempting to manipulate or influence an appraiser's evaluation of a property.

2. Being convicted of, or entering a plea of guilty or nolo contendere to, regardless of adjudication, any felony.
3. Having a loan originator, mortgage broker, or mortgage lender license, or the equivalent of such license, revoked in any jurisdiction.
4. Engaging in unfair, deceptive, or misleading advertising.

Maximum fines for violations of Chapter 494 have been increased to $25,000 for each count or separate offense. Persons who are guilty of unlicensed activity may be fined up to $1,000 per day to a maximum $25,000. The Office of Financial Regulation must report disciplinary actions to the NMLS.

Some penalties carry lifetime bans from licensure.

FORM 1004 APPRAISAL REPORT

During the run-up to the mortgage loan crisis, lenders did not have a uniform method to determine when the market conditions were changing. Many experts believe that greater transparency might have resulted in applying the brakes to many areas that were becoming overbuilt. In 2009, steps were taken to correct the problem, however belatedly.

All conventional appraisals dated on or after April 1, 2009, must include the Market Conditions Addendum to the Appraisal Report. The form allows the appraiser to detail local market condition information so that the lender has a better understanding of the market trends for the subject property. The addendum includes information about the absorption rate of homes in the neighborhood, the number of active listings, and the number of days on the market. The appraiser must show whether the trends are increasing, stable, or decreasing. The appraiser must also comment on trends in seller concessions (paying for closing costs, buydowns, etc.) for the previous 12 months. This form will help lenders to see emerging patterns that might call for greater caution.

HOME VALUATION CODE OF CONDUCT

Nearly 75 percent of residential mortgage appraisals are arranged through brokers who only get paid if the loan closes. This practice created a huge financial incentive for the brokers to pressure appraisers toward higher appraisals. Other unsound practices included:

- the practice of a sales associate or lender selecting the appraiser most likely to "hit the mark,"
- high pressure applied to appraisers by brokers or lenders to make the transaction work,
- demands by lenders to appraisers to have the appraiser provide value estimates or comparable sales before the appraisal is complete,
- lenders use of in-house appraisers, and
- requesting a second appraisal from another appraiser if the first property appraisal does not result in the value needed to close the sale.

Andrew Cuomo, the New York attorney general, has sued eAppraiseIt, an appraisal management firm because it caved in to pressure from Washington Mutual (WaMu) and illegally used a list of "proven" appraisers who provided inflated appraisals on homes. EA provided approximately 262,000 appraisals for WaMu.

Largely because of pressure from Cuomo, Fannie Mae and Freddie Mac have established the Home Valuation Code of Conduct, creating a "firewall" between the loan originators and appraisers. Effective May 1, 2009, lenders must represent and warrant that appraisals prepared in connection with mortgage loans conform to the Code. The Code was due to sunset November 1, 2010. The new Consumer Financial Protection Agency is likely to issue new rules to protect appraisers from lender pressure. The agency will also decide if the Code should be continued.

Major provisions of the Code are the following:

- No employee or agent of the lender shall influence or attempt to influence the appraiser through coercion, extortion, compensation, intimidation, or any other manner.
- Lenders cannot request a preliminary estimate of value or a list of comparable sales from an appraiser.
- Appraisers cannot be removed from a lenders "approved" list, except when the lender provides written notice of specific violations of USPAP.
- Lenders cannot order a second appraisal ("shop the appraisal") of the subject property without showing in the file the reasons why the first appraisal was flawed.
- Lenders must give borrowers a copy of the appraisal report at no charge.
- Lenders cannot control or own more than 20 percent of an appraisal management company.
- The lender shall not accept any appraisal paid for by any third party, such as a builder, or real estate broker, or settlement services provider.
- Lenders, originators, and any other person employed by the lender shall not select or communicate with the appraiser for the subject property, except to request additional information or to correct objective factual errors.
- Persons who select the appraiser for a loan transaction must be wholly independent of the loan production side of the business.

Appraisers no longer need fear being "blacklisted" from receiving work again, nor will they face such relentless pressure from lenders or real estate brokers.

NEW FHA APPRAISAL REQUIREMENTS

Effective April 1, 2009, FHA appraisers must now provide the following:

- The Market Conditions Addendum (Fannie Form 1004MC/Freddie Form 71)
- At least two comparable sales that occurred within 90 days of appraisal date
- A minimum of two active listings or pending sales in addition to the three closed comparables
- Bracketed listings using both dwelling size and sales price when possible
- Adjusted active listings to reflect the list-to-sales price ratio
- Adjusted pending sales to reflect contract sales price when possible
- The original list price and any revised list prices
- Reconciliation of adjusted values of active or pending sales with adjusted values of closed comparable sales
- Absorption rate analysis
- Known or reported sales concessions on active and pending sales

This update includes this warning: "Direct Endorsement Lenders are reminded that if the appraiser they selected provides a poor or fraudulent appraisal that leads FHA to insure a mortgage at an inflated amount, the lender is held responsible equally with the appraiser for the integrity, accuracy and thoroughness of an appraisal submitted to FHA."

CHANGES TO FLORIDA'S APPRAISAL LAW

In 2010, the Florida Legislature amended Chapter 475, Part II to establish regulation over appraisal management companies. These companies retain appraisers to perform appraisal services for clients, or act as intermediaries between clients and appraisers to facilitate the clients' contracting with appraisers.

Appraisal management companies must be registered with the DBPR. Owners, directors, officers or partners, depending on the type of entity, must be registered with the department and pass a criminal background check. All must sign a pledge to comply with the Uniform Standards of Professional Appraisal Practice (USPAP). These persons may not have had a registration or license to practice any profession denied or revoked.

For example, if Bayfront National Bank has taken a loan application, the bank may contact XYZ Appraisal Managers, Inc. arrange for the required appraisal for the loan. XYZ will then assign one or more appraisers from its appraisal panel to prepare the appraisal report. XYZ would violate the law if it:

- instructs an appraiser to violate the USPAP;
- accepts an appraisal assignment if the fee is contingent on a predetermined result;
- contracts with an appraiser whose license has been suspended or revokes; or
- attempts to influence the appraisal by:
  - withholding payment or future business,
  - promising future business,
  - conditioning a request for service based on a preliminary estimate from the appraiser,
  - requesting a preliminary valuation from the appraiser,
  - providing to the appraiser a desired value for a subject property,
  - allowing the removal of an appraiser from an appraiser panel without prior written notice, or
  - paying for a second appraisal without cause.

REAL ESTATE SETTLEMENT PROCEDURES ACT

The Real Estate Settlement Procedures Act (RESPA) was enacted in 1974 to protect buyers by requiring disclosure of the amounts and types of charges they must pay at closing. Transactions involving a federally related mortgage loan secured by a lien on residential property are covered by the act.

As a response to the financial crisis of 2008, the Department of Housing and Urban Development (HUD) amended Regulation X of the Act requiring compliance beginning January 1, 2010.

Following are the six principal areas of the RESPA as amended:

1. **Good-Faith Estimate (GFE):** The GFE must be given to the borrower at the time of loan application or within three business days after the receipt of the loan application. It itemizes estimated settlement costs. Effective January 1, 2010, the form was changed from a simple one-page form to a more informative three-page document. Among other things, the GFE now has certain tolerances for accuracy. Some of the costs quoted may not increase at settlement and other costs may increase no more than ten percent. Table 7.1 summarizes these costs.

TABLE 7.1 Summary of Good Faith Estimate Charges

These charges cannot increase at settlement	The total of these charges can increase up to 10% at settlement (Required services that the lender selects)	These charges can change at settlement (Required services that the borrower can shop for—if borrower does not use companies identified by lender)
Lender origination charge	Title services and lender's title insurance (if lender selects them or borrower uses companies lender identifies)	Title services and lender's title insurance (if borrower does not use companies lender identifies)
Borrower credit or charge (points) for the specific interest rate chosen (after borrower locks in interest rate)	Owner's title insurance (if borrower uses companies lender identifies)	Owner's title insurance (if borrower does not use companies lender identifies)
Borrower adjusted origination charges (after borrower locks in interest rate)	Required services that borrower can shop for (if borrower uses companies lender identifies)	Initial deposit for borrower escrow account
Transfer taxes	Government recording charges	Daily interest charges
		Homeowner's insurance

There is concern among many lenders that the new GFE is inferior to the one it replaced. Two very important items are missing from the form:

- Only the principal and interest portion of the mortgage payment is shown, not the total monthly mortgage payment (including taxes and insurance)
- Total settlement costs are shown, but not the total cash needed to close

Most lenders are filling in the gaps by giving borrowers a "worksheet" to provide the information. Interestingly, the worksheets are very similar to the old GFEs.

2. **Settlement Cost Booklet:** The booklet was updated to reflect the changes to the GFE and the HUD-1 Settlement Statement.
3. **Selection of the Closing Agent:** The lender must disclose the business relationship and the charges of any closing agent if the lender requires that the loan be closed by that agent.
4. **Purchase of Title Insurance:** A seller may not make it a condition of the sale that the buyer purchase title insurance from a particular company.
5. **No Kickbacks:** Service fees may not be paid unless a service was actually performed by a person licensed to do so, and all parties are informed. Referral fees between brokers are permitted.
6. **HUD-1 Uniform Settlement Statement:** The HUD-1 has been expanded from two pages to three pages. The section detailing the borrowers' costs shows the line numbers of the Good Faith Estimate to promote comparison. The new third page is a comparison chart of charges estimated by the lender on the GFE and the actual charges for the services as shown on the HUD-1. If any

of the charges on the HUD-1 form are higher than the allowed tolerances, the lender must refund the excess to the borrower within 30 days.

FLORIDA ANTI-KICKBACK LAWS

Related to RESPA rules, Florida vigorously enforces anti-kickback rules. It would be a serious violation if a title insurance agent did any of the following for a real estate licensee:

- Printing or paying for printing advertising materials
- Furnishing or paying for office equipment
- Providing or paying for cell phones
- Providing or paying for fuel for vehicles
- Sponsoring, hosting, or paying for open houses
- Paying real estate agents to fill out processing forms in exchange for contracts

TRUTH-IN-LENDING

The Truth-in-Lending Act (implemented by the Federal Reserve Board's Regulation Z) requires that creditors disclose the cost of borrowing in plain language so consumers can understand the charges, compare costs, and shop around for the best credit deal. This section covers Truth-in-Lending for residential mortgage loans.

The law also applies to real estate licensees who advertise credit terms to be granted by an institutional lender. When a licensee advertises certain information, called *triggers*, the licensee must disclose all the components of the financing.

For example, any of the following information in a real estate ad is a "trigger":

- The amount or percentage of the down payment (e.g., "5% down"; "$4,000 down")
- The amount or percentage of any payment ("payments $896.54 monthly")
- The number of payments or the period of repayment ("15-year or 30-year mortgages available")
- The amount of any finance charges ("less than $1,800 interest in year one")

Any "trigger" requires that the licensee disclose the following information:

- The amount or percentage of the down payment, which would normally show the purchase price, the down payment, and the amount financed
- The terms of repayment, which would normally show the payment amount and the number of payments required
- The annual percentage rate, using that term or the abbreviation "APR," taking into account the amount of the loan, timing of the payments, the finance charge, and the note rate

---

IN PRACTICE

Advertise Credit in General Terms

You can avoid making all the "triggered" disclosures if your advertising is couched in general, rather than specific, terms. For example, the following phrases do not trigger additional disclosures:

- No down payment
- Easy terms
- Biweekly payments

Disclosure of Annual Percentage Rate for New Mortgages

When mortgage lenders calculate the annual percentage rate of a loan, they must include not only interest, points, and origination fees but also many other buyer fees (such as amortization schedule, application fee, assignment fee, assumption fee, commitment fee, courier fee, funding fee, construction inspection fee, mortgage broker fee, mortgage insurance premiums, loan processing fees, recording fees, tax service fee, title endorsement fee, verification fee, and wire fee).

A basic rule for advertising credit is this: if the ad shows the finance charge as a rate, that rate must be stated as an "annual percentage rate" or "APR."

Penalties for Failure to Disclose

The Truth-in-Lending Act allows a consumer to sue an advertiser who fails to disclose all aspects of institutional credit financing.

PROGRESS QUIZ

36. The Truth-in-Lending Act requires lenders to
    a. disclose closing costs and prepaids within three business days of a borrower's application.
    b. show the cost of borrowing as an annual percentage rate.
    c. provide equal service to all applicants without discrimination based on a protected class.
    d. consider income from alimony, child support, or separate maintenance agreements.

THE EQUAL CREDIT OPPORTUNITY ACT

The Equal Credit Opportunity Act (ECOA) and the Fair Housing Act protect consumers against discrimination when they buy homes and apply for mortgages to purchase, refinance, or make home improvements. The Federal Trade Commission (FTC) and other federal agencies have enforcement responsibilities.

Consumer Rights Under ECOA

The ECOA prohibits discrimination in any aspect of a credit transaction based on the following:

- Race or color
- Religion
- National origin
- Sex
- Marital status
- Age (provided the applicant has the capacity to contract)
- The applicant's receipt of income derived from any public assistance program
- The applicant's exercise, in good faith, of any right under the Consumer Credit Protection Act, the umbrella statute that includes ECOA

Sources of Income That Lenders Must Consider

The law is very strict on the way lenders evaluate their customers' qualifications. Lenders must do the following:

- Consider reliable public assistance income in the same way as other income
- Consider reliable income from part-time employment, Social Security, pensions, and annuities

- Consider reliable alimony, child support, or separate maintenance payments. A lender may require proof that this income be consistent.
- Accept someone other than a spouse, if a cosigner is needed. If both spouses own the property, both may be required to sign mortgage documents, even if only one spouse must sign the note.
- Consider income regardless of sex or marital status. For example, a creditor cannot count a man's salary at 100 percent and a woman's at 75 percent. A creditor may not assume that a woman of childbearing age will stop working to raise children.

If Customers Suspect Discrimination

Consumers should take one of the following actions if they think they have been a victim of discrimination:

- Complain to the lender. Sometimes lenders can be persuaded to reconsider.
- Check with the state attorney general's office to see if the creditor violated state laws
- Contact a local private fair housing group and report violations to the appropriate government agency. If the mortgage application is denied, the lender must give the name and address of the agency to contact.
- Consider suing the lender in federal district court. If the court finds that a lender's conduct was willful, consumers can recover their actual damages and be awarded punitive damages. They also may recover reasonable legal fees and court costs. In addition, they might consider joining with others in a class action suit.

> For ECOA violations involving mortgage and consumer finance companies:
>
> Federal Trade Commission
> Consumer Response Center
> Washington, DC 20580
> 202-326-2222

Federal Enforcement

Many federal agencies share enforcement responsibility for the ECOA and the Fair Housing Act. Determining which agency to contact depends, in part, on the type of financial institution to which the applicant applied.

PROGRESS QUIZ

37. All these lender's actions are violations of the Equal Credit Opportunity Act EXCEPT
   a. refusing to consider public assistance income in the application.
   b. considering reliable income from part-time employment.
   c. refusing to consider reliable alimony payments as income.
   d. refusing to consider Social Security income.

FAIR CREDIT REPORTING

A credit file exists for people who have applied for a charge account, a personal loan, insurance, or a job. This file contains information on where they work and live, how they pay their bills, and whether they've been sued or arrested or have filed for bankruptcy.

Companies that gather and sell this information are called *Consumer Reporting Agencies* (CRAs). The most common type of CRA is the credit bureau. The information CRAs sell is called a *consumer report*.

Purpose of the Fair Credit Reporting Act

The Fair Credit Reporting Act (FCRA), enforced by the Federal Trade Commission, is designed to promote accuracy and ensure the privacy of the information used in consumer reports. Recent amendments to the act expand consumer rights and place additional requirements on CRAs. Businesses that supply information to CRAs and those that use consumer reports also have new responsibilities under the law.

Major National Credit Bureaus

To find the CRA that has a report, a consumer should contact the CRAs listed in the Yellow Pages under "Credit" or "Credit Rating and Reporting." Each should be called until all the agencies maintaining the consumer's file have been found. The three major national credit bureaus are:

- Equifax, P.O. Box 105873, Atlanta, GA 30348; 800-685-1111
- Experian, P.O. Box 2002, Allen, TX 75013; 800-397-3742
- TransUnion, 2 Baldwin Place, Chester, PA 19022; 800-888-4213

In addition, anyone who takes action against a consumer in response to a report supplied by a CRA—such as denying an application for credit, insurance, or employment—must give the consumer the name, address, and telephone number of the CRA that provided the report.

Consumers have certain rights:

 **Web.Link**

- The right to get a free copy of their credit reports each year to verify that the correct information is reported. Consumers may go to the official Web site at *www.annualcreditreport.com/cra/index.jsp* to get their report.
- The right to inspect their report and get a list of everyone who has requested a report within the past year (two years for employment-related requests). There is no charge for the report requested if a company takes adverse action against the applicant, such as denying an application for credit, insurance, or employment, and the report is requested within 60 days of receiving the notice of the action.
- Both the CRA and the information provider must correct inaccurate or incomplete information in a credit report. The consumer must contact both the CRA and the information provider.

PROGRESS QUIZ

38. An applicant who has been turned down for a loan does NOT have the right to
    a. get the name, address, and telephone number of the consumer reporting agency that provided the credit report.
    b. find out what is in the credit report at no charge.
    c. get a list of everyone who has requested a report within the past year.
    d. receive a refund of the application fee.

Length of Time Credit Information Is Retained in a File

A CRA may report negative information for seven years. There are certain exceptions:

- Information about criminal convictions may be reported without any time limitation.
- Bankruptcy information may be reported for ten years.
- Information reported in response to an application for a job with a salary of more than $75,000 has no time limit.
- Information reported because of an application for more than $150,000 worth of credit or life insurance has no time limit.
- Information about a lawsuit or an unpaid judgment against the consumer can be reported for the longer of seven years or until the statute of limitations expires.

PROGRESS QUIZ

39. Which statement is correct about the length of time information may be retained in a person's credit report?
    a. Information about criminal convictions may be reported for only seven years.
    b. Information about a lawsuit or unpaid judgment may be reported for seven years or until the statute of limitations runs out, whichever is later.
    c. Information about bankruptcies may be reported for seven years.
    d. Information in response to a job application with a salary of more than $75,000 has a ten-year time limit.

Credit Scoring

A major reason Fannie Mae and Freddie Mac lenders are willing to make immediate loan decisions is credit scoring. Credit scoring uses statistical samples to predict how likely it is that a borrower will pay back a loan. To develop a model, the lender selects a large random sample of its borrowers, analyzing characteristics that relate to creditworthiness. Each of the characteristics is assigned a weight, based on how strong a predictor it is. Credit scores treat each person objectively because the same standards apply to everyone. Credit scores are blind to demographic or cultural differences among people.

The most commonly used credit score today is known as a "FICO" score, named after the company that developed it, Fair Isaac Corp. FICO scores range from 400 to 900. The lower the score, the greater the risk of default.

According to FICO, a person's score consists of the following components:

- 35 percent of the score is determined by payment histories on credit accounts, with recent history weighted a bit more heavily than the distant past.
- 30 percent is based on the amount of debt outstanding with all creditors.
- 15 percent is produced on the basis of how long the borrower has been a credit user (a longer history is better if there have always been timely payments).
- 10 percent is comprised of very recent history and whether the borrower has been actively seeking (and getting) loans or credit lines in the past months.
- 10 percent is calculated from the mix of credit held, including installment loans (like car loans), leases, mortgages, credit cards, and so on.

How to increase a personal credit score. Increasing one's personal credit score is a long-term process. Some of the most important steps to a better credit score are listed here:

- Pay bills on time. Late payments and collections can have a serious impact on the FICO score.
- Do not apply for credit frequently. Having a large number of inquiries shown on your credit report can lower the score.
- Reduce credit card balances. Persons who are "maxed out" will find their score declines.
- Be certain to obtain enough credit to establish a credit history. Not having sufficient credit can negatively impact the score.

Freddie Mac has found that borrowers with credit scores above 660 are likely to repay the mortgage, and underwriters can do basic reviews of the files for completeness. For applicants with scores between 620 and 660, the underwriter is required to do a comprehensive review. A very cautious review would be made for persons with credit scores below 620.

Another important scoring system, VantageScore, was introduced in 2006 by the three credit-reporting agencies: Equifax, Experian, and TransUnion. All three use the same formula to calculate the score, unlike the FICO system, wherein each credit bureau uses a different formula. The formula differences are slight. The VantageScore system grades from "A" (best) through "F." More than 200 lenders are currently testing VantageScore as a primary scoring method, but none have switched from FICO yet. FICO's stock price dropped 6 percent the day VantageScore was announced. The credit bureaus will profit most if the new standard becomes generally accepted.

Borrowers who are quoted higher-than-market rates should shop among many lenders for the best terms. If borrowers had access to their scores and more knowledge of the lending process, they could obtain better loans. In this endeavor, a real estate licensee can be very helpful.

While most consumers have full credit bureau reports used by lenders to evaluate credit risks, approximately 54 million Americans (young people, recent immigrants, or newly divorced or widowed consumers) have no reports on file. Because these situations make it difficult to qualify for mortgages, FICO has developed a new credit score program that lenders may elect to use. This program evaluates "nontraditional" data, such as how well consumers handled payday loans and retail payment plans. The FICO score will also review how responsibly individuals used their checking accounts' overdraft protections.

@ Web.Link   H.S.H. Associates, financial publishers: mortgage information: *www.hsh.com*

Is credit scoring valid? With credit scoring, lenders can evaluate millions of applicants consistently and impartially on many different characteristics. To be statistically valid, the system must be based on a big enough sample. When properly designed, the system promotes fast, impartial decisions.

FICO has recently completed NextGen, designed to more precisely define the risk of borrowers because it analyzes more criteria than the old model. Using the new model, lenders can evaluate credit profiles of high-risk borrowers in terms of degrees, rather than combining them into the same category.

What are the future uses of credit scoring? Many experts believe that residential lending will begin to use credit scoring the same way it is used in automobile financing and consumer loans. Freddie Mac is currently conducting a pilot program with large lenders. Interest rates on home mortgages may be based on the credit score. Today's "6 percent mortgage" may be tomorrow's "5¾ percent for A+ borrowers, 6 percent for A, and 6¼ percent for B+."

HOMEOWNERS PROTECTION ACT OF 1998

Conventional lenders usually require that a borrower who makes less than a 20 percent down payment pay for private mortgage insurance (PMI). PMI protects the lender if the borrower defaults on the loan. The Homeowners Protection Act of 1998, which became effective in 1999, established rules for automatic termination and borrower cancellation of PMI on home mortgages. These protections apply to certain home mortgages signed on or after July 29, 1999. These protections do not apply to government-insured FHA or VA loans or to loans with lender-paid PMI.

For home mortgages signed on or after July 29, 1999, PMI must, with certain exceptions, be terminated automatically when the borrower has achieved 22 percent equity in the home based on the original property value, if the mortgage payments are current. PMI also can be canceled, when the borrower requests it—with certain exceptions—when the borrower achieves 20 percent equity in the home based on the original property value, if the mortgage payments are current.

The PMI may continue if:

- the loan is "high-risk,"
- the borrower has not been current on the payments within the year prior to the time for termination or cancellation, or
- the borrower has other liens on the property.

The FHA Home Buyer Savings Plan has also reduced mortgage insurance premiums on loans originated after January 1, 2001, from 2.25 percent to 1.5 percent of the original loan amount. FHA has also eliminated the 0.5 percent annual premium for borrowers who have achieved 22 percent equity in their house, based on the lower of the purchase price or the appraisal.

OTHER TRENDS IN FINANCING REAL PROPERTY

The mortgage market is changing as rapidly as many other sectors of the real estate industry, and technology is the engine of the change. Almost immediate loan approval is possible on the Web. Credit scoring will change the way mortgage interest rates are quoted. Appraisers can make restricted "drive-by" appraisals when a loan application is strong.

FHA Relaxes Its Lending Guidelines

As of January 1, 2007, appraisers have an easier time making appraisals for FHA-insured mortgages. Previously, there were five pages called VC (value condition) that appraisers had to check off, but the list was pared down. FHA is now only concerned with major problems such as structural damage, poor access to interior rooms, or standing water around a foundation.

In addition, FHA has changed its financing requirements by allowing buyers to be charged for any closing costs that are typical for the area. Previously, sellers were required to pay some of those costs, making sellers unwilling to accept offers that had FHA financing.

FHA also relaxed its ratio guidelines for manually underwritten loans. The maximum housing expense ratio is now 31 percent, and the maximum total obligations ratio is now 43 percent. Former ratios were 29 percent and 41 percent, respectively.

The new FHASecure plan allows families with strong credit histories who had been making timely mortgage payments before their loans reset—but are now in default—to qualify for refinancing. The combination of FHASecure and risk-based premium pricing lets FHA help stabilize the housing market and reduce the cycle of foreclosures. The plan will operate under the same safe guidelines as the FHA's existing mortgage insurance program without affecting FHA's financial health. Eligible homeowners will be required to meet strict underwriting guidelines and pay a mortgage insurance premium that offsets the risk to FHA's insurance fund at no cost to the taxpayer.

To qualify for FHASecure, homeowners must meet the following five criteria:

- A history of on-time mortgage payments before the borrower's teaser rates expired and loans reset
- Interest rates must have or will reset between June 2005 and December 2008
- Three percent cash or equity in the home
- A sustained history of employment
- Sufficient income to make the mortgage payment

Because of the new programs, FHA loans are expected to grow in popularity.

SHORT SALES

Many homeowners are already, or will soon be, in default on their mortgages. Prices in many areas have declined below the amount due to the mortgage lender, so owners have become economically "trapped," having to pay money (they don't have) to the lender at the time of refinancing or sale.

Because lenders would rather not have an empty, shuttered home, many are trying to work with borrowers who want to refinance or sell. The most common vehicle is called a "short sale." In a short sale, the lender agrees to accept less than the total amount due so that the house can be sold. This will not automatically release the borrower from liability under the note, however, and the borrower may later be forced to repay the deficiency.

Not all owners will qualify for a short sale. If the lender sees that the borrower has adequate income (or assets) to continue making payments on the loan, the lender is unlikely to take a loss on the mortgage. Different lenders have different requirements, but most will demand documentation from the borrower before agreeing to discount the mortgage.

@ Web.Link

Fannie Mae home page: *www.fanniemae.com*

Freddie Mac home page: *www.freddiemac.com*

FHA Single Family Insurance page: *www.huduser.org/publications/hsgfin/singlefa.html*

Federal Reserve Board: *www.federalreserve.gov*

U.S. Federal Trade Commission: *www.ftc.gov*

U.S. Department of Veterans Affairs: *www.va.gov*

IN PRACTICE

Steps to a Short Sale

Real estate professionals working with a borrower who needs a short sale to be able to sell should keep the following in mind:

- Start the process early in the listing period. It takes weeks or even months to get the documentation prepared and submitted and to get an indication from the lender that a short sale will be considered. Send the lender a letter detailing the borrower's name, property address, the loan number, your name, and an authorization letter (see more below).

- A part of this letter should detail reasons for the borrower's hardship. Loss of job or medical expenses are grounds for the lender to agree to help. Dishonesty on the original application about the borrower's income will not be helpful.

- Have the borrower give the lender written authorization to talk with you, the closing agent, and the new lender about the borrower's personal information. Without the authorization, the process will be more difficult, as you won't get much information from the lender.

- Give the lender a copy of your CMA and a preliminary seller's net statement. If the bottom line shows there will be cash from the sale, the lender is unlikely to discount the mortgage. If there is a shortage, that will be what you want the lender to discount.

- The lender wants assurance that the borrower can't pay the money back, so the borrower will need to send verifiable proof of assets and income, including copies of bank statements. Large recent withdrawals should be explained. The borrower may be asked to sign an affidavit that the information provided is complete and accurate.

- Carefully disclose in your listing information, the MLS, and to all buyers that there is no guarantee that the lender will agree to any price or terms for less than the mortgage amount.

- When an offer is submitted on the property, the lender will want a copy of the contract, the seller's net statement, and your listing agreement. You may be asked to discount your commission, or the lender may refuse to pay for expenses that are not standard.

- Prepare the seller and the buyer for a long process. Because the process can be slow, a buyer who has not been previously warned may want to get out of the contract and select another home.

Case Study

A SALES ASSOCIATE'S CREATIVE AD ATTRACTS BUYERS

● **Facts:** Prospective buyers responded to an ad promoting homes in "Beautiful Oak Grove Estates" with statements of "$1 down moves you in" and "all closing costs paid." The words "Call Dave" were shown at the bottom of the advertisement. When the buyers contracted to purchase a home, Dave, a licensed sales associate, required a deposit of $500, even though the ad stated that only one dollar was needed to close. Sales Associate Dave said their $499 would be returned at closing, and that was shown in the contract.

Dave told the buyers they could get their mortgage with Farmer's Loan. The buyers said there was an income cap on those loans, but Dave assured them there would be no problem. The buyers were not approved for the loan and had to get financing from another source.

Before closing, the buyers learned that Dave would not be returning the $499 because of higher costs from the new lender. The buyers agreed to close only after Sales Associate Dave promised to have a specific model garage door opener installed. After the buyers moved in, the wrong door opener was installed. After they complained, the door opener was removed and not replaced.

● **Questions:**

1. Do you believe Sales Associate Dave violated the law?

   _____
   _____
   _____

2. What sections of Chapter 475, F.S., did Sales Associate Dave violate?

   _____
   _____
   _____

3. What should Sales Associate Dave's punishment be?

   _____
   _____
   _____

● **Determination of Violation:** The administrative law judge prepared a recommended order to the Florida Real Estate Commission finding that Sales Associate Dave violated Sections 475.25(1)(b) and (c), Florida Statutes, by falsely advertising property or services, and by committing fraud, concealment, and dishonest dealing in a business transaction.

● **Penalty:** The Florida Real Estate Commission accepted the recommended order, imposing a fine of $1,000 and requiring a 45-hour sales associate post-licensing course.

Chapter 8

Contracts and Closing

In This Chapter

The statute of frauds ● Unauthorized practice of law ● Licensee acting as a buyer or seller ● Disclosures ● Florida sales tax on personal property ● Sales contracts ● Closing real estate transactions ● Closing procedures from the title company's perspective ● Evidence of title ● The title search ● At the closing table

Your Quick Reference Guide to the Major Changes in Contracts and Closings

Important changes you should carefully review:

● Murder, suicide, or death in a property no longer need be disclosed.

● New HUD rule on transaction fees; brokers must be cautious.

Learning Objectives

When you have completed this chapter, you should be able to:

● describe the contracts covered by the statute of frauds that must be written and signed to be enforceable,

● list the documents a licensee can prepare without practicing law,

● describe the steps law enforcement must take to meet Megan's Law requirements,

● state the time for disclosing transaction processing fees,

● describe how to include personal property in a contract to avoid sales tax liability,

● list at least five steps the licensee can take to reduce problems at closing,

● list the three major items to bring to the title closing agent when placing the title insurance order,

● list at least three exclusions or exceptions to a title insurance policy,

- explain why the Truth-in-Lending disclosure of an annual percentage rate may be different from the interest rate in a note, and

- explain the problems faced by title insurance companies that disburse funds at the time of closing.

THE STATUTE OF FRAUDS

Before the doctrine of the statute of frauds was accepted, it was not uncommon for a person to pay "witnesses" to falsify testimony to support a nonexistent oral contract for the sale of real property. The *statute of frauds* requires that certain types of contracts, to be enforceable, be in writing and be signed by all parties. Contracts required to be in writing and signed are of two general types: those that will not be performed within a short time and those that deal with specific subjects.

To be enforceable in Florida, an agreement or promise that cannot be performed by both parties within one year after the contract date must be written. Also, an agreement to sell or the actual sale of any interest in real property must be in writing and must be signed by all parties bound by the contract.

Two common exceptions to the statute of frauds are recognized: (1) if an oral contract has been completed, or (2) if the buyer has given a down payment and either moved in or made repairs. A sales contract is valid if the transaction has been closed and a deed delivered, as it clearly shows the intent of the parties.

PROGRESS QUIZ

40. Bill owned a small house in Pompano that he orally agreed to sell to Jane. She gave Bill a $2,000 good-faith deposit, and Bill allowed her to move in before the closing. Several weeks later, they argued about an unrelated matter, so Bill refused to go through with the sale of the property and gave Jane notice to vacate immediately. Jane sued to require him to sell. How will the court most likely rule?
    a. Jane must move out because the contract was not written and signed; therefore, the contract is unenforceable.
    b. Bill may have Jane evicted if she fails to move within a reasonable time.
    c. Because Jane made a down payment and moved in, the contract is enforceable.
    d. Bill is entitled to collect triple rent for the period Jane has been in the property after receiving notice to vacate.

UNAUTHORIZED PRACTICE OF LAW

Real estate licensees, in the course of their businesses, may prepare listing agreements, buyer's representation agreements, sales contracts, option contracts, and Florida Supreme Court–approved lease agreements that are for no longer than one year. The licensee and the licensee's employer may be legally responsible for errors. Licensees, when drafting special clauses not included in a preprinted contract, must recognize their liability if a clause is later found to be defective. To reduce the incidence of errors, many special clauses are available in forms developed by private brokerage firms and professional real estate associations.

Preparing documents such as deeds, notes, or mortgages would be considered unauthorized practice of law. A licensee who advertised to prepare or review sales contracts for persons not buying through the licensee might also be accused of practicing law.

41. Broker Jackson places an advertisement in the Miami Tribune reading: "Selling your own property? Have a Florida real estate broker prepare or review the deed and mortgage! $300 to prepare a deed and mortgage, or $150 for a review of all documents. Call William Jackson, broker, at 555-4507." Broker Jackson
    a. may do this service as advertised.
    b. is guilty of misrepresentation and fraud.
    c. is guilty of unauthorized practice of law.
    d. has run a blind ad.

LICENSEE ACTING AS A BUYER OR SELLER

Licensees often buy and sell property for their own accounts. Licensees who buy their own listing have substantial exposure to charges of misrepresentation. The licensee has probably helped the seller establish a listing price. The licensee has, therefore, acquired confidential information about the motivation of the seller and must act fairly when purchasing the property. The parties now have opposing interests in the transaction. The licensee must tell the seller any known information about the property and should say in the contract that the licensee does not represent the seller. A licensee may accept a commission in the transaction if the buyer or seller gives informed consent.

A licensee who buys property for a personal account and shows a good-faith deposit in the contract must comply with the FREC requirements for such deposits.

DISCLOSURES

Property Condition

When selling real property, sellers and licensees must reveal all known facts that materially affect the value of residential property that are not readily observable to the buyer. Some licensees work under the theory of "don't ask, don't tell." This can be the recipe for a lawsuit.

Forms to Go

To protect the parties to a contract and to reduce their liability, licensees should use a Seller's Real Property Disclosure Statement similar to the one shown in the Forms-To-Go section. This disclosure is a detailed fact sheet about a property, prepared and signed by the seller and given to a buyer before the contract is signed. The seller describes any defects in the property that may affect its value. The licensee should avoid helping the seller prepare this form.

Residential Property Issues Concerning Death or HIV/AIDS

Residential licensees have long debated the need to make disclosures when a murder, suicide, or death occurs in a house. The property is said to be *stigmatized* or *psychologically impacted*. Changes to Chapter 689 (Conveyances of Land and Declarations of Trust) now settle the matter; disclosure is not required.

New

The fact that a property was, or was at any time suspected to have been, the site of a homicide, suicide, or death is not a material fact that must be disclosed in a real estate transaction. A cause of action shall not arise against an owner of real property, the owner's agent, an agent of a transferee of real property, or a person licensed under Chapter 475 for the failure to disclose to the transferee that the property was or was suspected to have been the site of a homicide, suicide, or death or that an occupant of the property was infected with human immunodeficiency virus (HIV) or diagnosed with acquired immune deficiency syndrome (AIDS). [689.25(1)(b)]

Megan's Law

Megan's Law is named for seven-year-old Megan Kanka of Hamilton Township, New Jersey. A convicted sex offender who lived across the street from Megan's family killed the girl. Her family was unaware of his past. In May 1996, a federal law was passed requiring that public law enforcement agencies register and disclose the addresses of convicted sex offenders. On July 1, 1996, Chapter 97.299, F.S., required that the Florida Department of Law Enforcement (FDLE) maintain an updated list of registered sexual predators in this state.

The law does not require that licensees disclose the addresses of convicted sex offenders. While the licensee could possibly be sued for failure to reveal such information, providing outdated or wrong information could also result in substantial liability. The FDLE cautions that positive identification of a person believed to be a sexual predator or sex offender cannot be established unless a fingerprint comparison is made.

Some licensees may wish to use a disclosure statement that recommends that buyers contact local law enforcement agencies for the information. A sample disclosure is shown below.

MEGAN'S LAW DISCLOSURE

Megan's Law is legislation designed to protect the public by notifying communities when a convicted sex offender moves into an area. Information including photos, identities, and addresses is available from the Florida Department of Law Enforcement (FDLE) at (850) 410-7000, or on the Internet at the site shown in the following Web link.

The buyer is encouraged to contact the FDLE for further information.

 **Web.Link**

FDLE's List of Registered Sexual Predators: *www.fdle.state.fl.us*

Transaction Fees

Many real estate firms employ personnel to facilitate transaction closings and charge additional fees, called *transaction fees*, *closing fees*, or something similar. Such fees may range from $25 to $500, in addition to real estate commissions paid by customers. Charging a transaction fee is a business decision properly made by each brokerage firm and does not conflict with the license law.

> **Disclose Transaction Processing Fees!**
>
> In a case involving nondisclosure of a transaction processing fee, the Commission imposed a $1,000 fine and a reprimand against a brokerage firm for failing to disclose the fee to a seller when taking a listing. The fee was included in the seller's net statement, but the FREC said the disclosure came too late.

Because many consumers make decisions on brokerage relationships partly based on the amount of fees charged, disclosure of such fees should be made before a seller signs a listing agreement or before showing property to a buyer. Disclosure of the fee just before the buyer signs the sales contract is too late.

In October 2001, HUD published a statement of policy that does not automatically make transaction fees a violation of RESPA but sets guidelines that must be followed. Brokers who charge transaction fees should be very cautious. There are now significant limitations on the amounts of such transaction fees as well as a defined test, which must be satisfied in order to avoid a violation of RESPA.

The National Association of REALTORS® engaged a prominent RESPA attorney, Phillip J. Schulman, to review the HUD Statement of Policy. Schulman recommended to members of the NAR that brokers who charge a transaction fee adhere to the following guidelines:

- The fee may not be excessive and must bear a direct relationship to the additional services or functions performed by the real estate broker.
- The fee must be for actual services rendered.
- A real estate broker MAY NOT charge or collect a transaction fee that is simply an add-on to the transaction with the consumer and has no direct relationship to work performed. In accordance with HUD's Statement of Policy, the charging and collection of administrative fees where no work or services are provided, or where such work or services are nominal in nature or duplicative, are violations of RESPA.
- The charging and collection of such fees must be fully disclosed to the consumer. The best practice is to disclose in the listing agreement that the commission will be, for example "6% + $250" so that the amounts show on one line in the HUD-1 form at closing. If they are on different lines, the licensee may have to justify the fees and show substantial work was done.

FLORIDA SALES TAX ON PERSONAL PROPERTY

The Florida Department of Revenue has made several rulings on the sales tax liability of personal property included in the sale of real property. If itemized in the sales contract, with a separately stated value for each item, sales tax must be paid. No sales tax is due, however, if the contract simply lists the property, such as a "refrigerator, range, microwave, and washer/dryer combination." Obviously, licensees should not itemize separately with stated values unless there are good reasons for doing so.

PROGRESS QUIZ

42. Sales tax liability is triggered on a real estate purchase contract when personal property is
    a. described in a contract.
    b. itemized and a separate value for each item placed in the contract.
    c. said to add value.
    d. said to be left for the convenience of the parties.

SALES CONTRACTS

A *sales contract* is a written agreement containing the terms for the transfer of real property and requires the signatures of all parties to the agreement.

Whether to Use a Printed Form

The Florida Association of REALTORS® and the Florida Bar Association jointly developed a standard residential contract form called the FAR/BAR Contract for Sale and Purchase. Also, the Florida Association of REALTORS® has developed the Residential Purchase and Sale Contract. These two contracts are the most widely used in Florida and are intended for use in routine transactions involving the sale of single-family dwellings or vacant land. Other transactions, such as the sales of businesses, construction, or lease options, usually require contracts specifically designed for that purpose.

Responsibility for Preparation

A sales contract is a bilateral contract and should express the complete intent of the parties. It must be prepared with skill, care, and diligence, a duty of single agents and transaction brokers. If a licensee is not certain about the contract or wording for any special clause, the safest action is to consult an experienced real estate attorney.

The licensee who prepares the contract and the licensee's employer are responsible for any mistakes in the agreement. If any errors, omissions, or ambiguities exist regarding material terms, the courts will not go outside the contents of the contract to decide intent. The licensee who prepared the contract will not be allowed to explain later an intent not shown in the contents of the contract. If a contract is vague and found unenforceable, the result could be a lost transaction, disciplinary action, and a civil lawsuit against the licensee.

Deposit

If a contract calls for an additional deposit, the amount and the number of days within which it is to be made should be inserted. If the buyer fails to make the additional deposit, it is a default, and the seller may recover not only the initial deposit but also any unpaid deposit. It is the licensee's duty to notify the seller promptly and follow the seller's directions.

FREC's time limits for depositing funds must be followed.

Disclosure Riders

Contract "riders" are additions or disclosures given when circumstances dictate. Various laws and regulations require that some riders be attached to the contracts.

Condominium rider. Because the printed clauses of the contract do not contain any specific provisions relating to the sale and purchase of condominium units, this rider should be attached to the contract. It addresses the condominium association's approval of the buyer, payment of assessments and special assessments, and delivery of condominium documents.

VA/FHA rider. Because transactions involving VA or FHA financing include many unique elements, the standard provisions of the FAR/BAR contract conflict with the requirements of the lender in an FHA/VA transaction. Consequently, attachment of the rider is a necessity when FHA or VA financing is involved.

Homeowners' association disclosure. This disclosure rider should be given to the buyer if there is a homeowners' association that can place a lien on the property for nonpayment of homeowners' dues or has restrictive covenants regulating the use and occupancy of the property. If the licensee does not provide the disclosure or if the contract does not have the required notice, the buyer may cancel the contract within three days or before closing, whichever comes first. See Chapter 3 for more details.

"As-is" rider. This is the buyer's agreement to take the property with no warranties about its condition. The rider does not relieve licensees or the seller of the duty to disclose material defects that affect the value of the property.

Lead-based paint rider. This disclosure is required for all homes built before 1978.

Coastal construction control line (CCCL) rider. The seller must provide a buyer, at or before closing, an affidavit or a survey delineating the CCCL location. The buyer may waive this requirement, but the waiver must be in writing. See Chapter 3 for more information.

Insulation rider. The Federal Trade Commission requires this rider when the sale involves new residential improved real property. It must show the insulation having been installed or to be installed in walls, ceilings, and other areas.

Additional Disclosures Required

The following written disclosures are also required: radon gas, energy efficiency, and tax treatment of foreign sellers (FIRPTA).

Comprehensive Buyer's Disclosures

Real estate associations as well as brokerage firms have prepared Comprehensive Buyer's Disclosures with many or all of the required riders on one page. This simplifies the contract and reduces paperwork. A sample is included in the Forms-To-Go section.

CLOSING REAL ESTATE TRANSACTIONS

Once the real estate contract has been signed, the licensee's work has just begun. The parties to a transaction expect their sales associate personally to monitor and coordinate all the details of their closing. While the licensee may believe the "torch has been passed" to the next group of professionals (lenders and closing agents), the buyer and seller continue to look to the real estate professional to coordinate all the details of the transaction. A smooth transition from contract to closing enhances the reputations of the firm and the sales associate. This section is intended to help licensees better understand the process. (See Figure 8.1.)

Some important steps a licensee may take to reduce problems with title closing include the following:

- Disclosing everything to all parties that will affect their decisions before the buyer and seller sign the contract. Surprises after a contract is signed almost certainly will result in one party wanting to get out of the contract.
- Writing the contract carefully and properly explaining it to the parties
- Recommending that buyers and sellers select lenders and title closing agents who are organized professionals able to meet deadlines
- Telling the loan processor and closing agent what the licensee expects in the way of communication and performance

- Preparing a property sale information form similar to the one shown in the Forms-To-Go section
- Giving the closing agent a copy of the prior title insurance policy, if possible
- Providing a complete legal description of the property to the closing agent
- Asking a lender and title agent to communicate by e-mail, speeding the process, while also providing written documentation of the transaction
- Using a checklist of duties, such as the Closing Progress Chart shown in the Forms-To-Go section
- Asking the closing agent to close the buyer's and seller's sides separately to reduce confusion during the closing

CLOSING PROCEDURES FROM THE TITLE COMPANY'S PERSPECTIVE

Real estate licensees who understand the title closing process are better able to serve their customers and clients. Knowledgeable licensees anticipate which documents and information the closing agent will need and have them ready when the title order is placed.

FIGURE 8.1 The Road to Closing

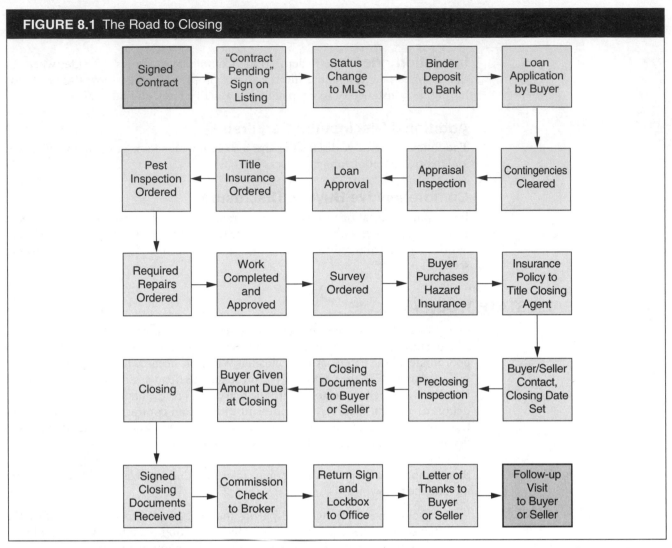

Source: *Post-Licensing Education for Real Estate Sales Associates*, Sixth Edition, by Edward J. O'Donnell, Dearborn Real Estate Education, Chicago, 2005.

Opening the File

Title closing agents would like to receive the following items when a title insurance order is placed:

- A properly signed and dated sales contract
- A previous title insurance policy on the property
- Enough information about the sellers, buyers, property, and lender to process and close the transaction, including:
  - the sellers' and buyers' marital status,
  - a complete legal description (e.g., lot, block, subdivision name, unit, recording information, and county),
  - street address including zip code,
  - terms of any purchase-money mortgage the title company must prepare,
  - closing date and information about whether all parties will attend or whether the documents must be mailed for signature, and
  - commission to the broker and information on commission splits between brokers.

Ordering the Title Search

The closing agent, after ensuring that all necessary information is in the file, will then order a *title search*. The following section includes more information on Florida land titles.

EVIDENCE OF TITLE

There are two principal methods for giving evidence of title to a buyer: (1) abstract or (2) title insurance. An attorney uses the *abstract* to give an *opinion of title*.

Abstract

An *abstract* summarizes the material parts of all recorded documents affecting title to property in chronological order. In the strict sense of the word, abstracting is becoming a lost art. With the development of microfilm, photocopying, computers, and the Internet, copies of the actual document can be inspected.

Opinion of Title

An *opinion of title* is an attorney's professional opinion of the condition of title, based on examination of the recorded documents pertaining to the property. If the title to the subject property is later found defective, the buyer may find it difficult to be reimbursed for damages unless the attorney was negligent in the search.

Today, attorneys acting as closing agents order title insurance just as a title company does.

Title Insurance

The reason title insurance has become the dominant method of protection for buyers and lenders is that it will pay for losses sustained by the new owner or the lender; the new owner does not have to prove negligence. The two basic types of title insurance are owners' title insurance and lenders' title insurance.

Like most insurance policies, there are exclusions and exceptions from the insurance. These arise mainly from government restrictions on ownership (police power, eminent domain, and ad valorem taxation) and private restrictions (deed restrictions).

Exclusions

A title insurance policy does not cover:

- Police power of the government, such as zoning, building restrictions, setback requirements, and so on
- Rights of eminent domain
- Liens or encumbrances created by the insured person, or known to the insured person at the time of purchase, but not known by the title insurance company
- Liens or encumbrances attaching to the property after the policy date

Exceptions

Typical policy exceptions include:

- the rights of a party in possession of the property that are not shown in the public records, such as a rental tenant;
- encroachments that could have been found if a survey had been made;
- easements not shown in the public records, such as an old roadway on the property (prescriptive easement);
- construction lien rights not shown in the public record;

- ad valorem taxes or special assessments not shown as existing liens; and
- restrictive covenants.

ALTA Title Policies

Exactly which defects are covered under the insurance depends on the type of insurance policy. A *standard coverage policy* normally insures the title as it is known from the public records. It also insures against such hidden defects as forged documents, conveyance by incompetent grantors, incorrect marital statements, and improperly delivered deeds. An *extended coverage policy*, such as an American Land Title Association (ALTA) policy, gives more coverage. For instance, it will protect against defects that may be discovered by a property inspection, rights of parties in possession, examination of a survey, and certain unrecorded liens. Most lenders require a lender's ALTA policy.

ALTA's expanded coverage policies cost about 10 percent more, but offer significantly more benefits. For example, the policies will pay up to 125 percent of the original insurance amount in case of claims to help account for inflation. Other expanded coverages include:

- encroachments on the land made by neighbors after the date of the policy,
- inability to access the property by vehicle or a pedestrian, and
- zoning violations made by previous owners that must be corrected by the insured owner.

@ Web.Link   Complete list of the expanded coverage benefits: *www.alta.org/forms*

PROGRESS QUIZ

43. Which is included in an extended coverage title insurance policy that would NOT be included in a standard coverage policy?
    a. Unrecorded liens not known of by the policyholder
    b. Forged documents
    c. Incorrect marital statements
    d. Improperly delivered deeds

THE TITLE SEARCH

The title searcher must review all the instruments, conveyances, public records, and court proceedings to discover any material facts related to the title of a property. The searcher is ensuring that the chain of title is intact.

Additionally, the searcher will be careful to see that all encumbrances, such as liens, have been or will be satisfied at closing. When insuring title, the searcher wants to be certain that the claims of any other person are extinguished, or, if not extinguished, that the buyer agrees to take title subject to those encumbrances.

The buyers' names must also be checked in the records to be certain there are no judgment liens against the buyers that would "jump" onto the title immediately after recording the deed but before the mortgage could be recorded.

For an in-house examination, a title agent prepares a search sheet with copies of instruments from public records. When the *title commitment* is typed, it must be carefully reviewed to see that names and legal descriptions match those on the contract and that amounts are correct. If a prior title policy is available, it must be checked to see that any exceptions are carried forward to the new commitment. The buyers receive only a commitment prior to closing. The complete title insurance policy is issued after the documents have been recorded.

Preparing to Close

The closing agent must send for mortgage payoff letters and check with public authorities for information on taxes and special assessments.

Loan Package

The lender normally sends documents and closing instructions in a loan package. The loan documents are checked for names, legal descriptions, and loan amounts. The title closing agent must follow the lender's instructions exactly, or the agent may be contractually liable to the lender for hundreds of dollars per day until the corrections are made.

The HUD-1 Settlement Statement

The closing agent should prepare and distribute a copy of the HUD-1 closing statement before closing. The title closing agent must certify that the statement is a true and accurate statement of the transaction, and that funds will be disbursed according to the statement. Huge fines have been assessed against closing agents who showed receipts of nonexistent deposits or of payments being made but not shown on the statement. Many title companies require an affidavit from the buyer, seller, and real estate licensee that there are no hidden mortgages, borrowed closing funds, or any other "under the table" agreements.

Scheduling the Closing

The closing agent must notify the parties of the date and time of closing. Most licensees prefer to be notified by the closing agent but want to tell their buyers or sellers directly. The amount due from the buyer should be in a certified check to speed disbursement. The closing agent will check with the licensee for any tasks that still need to be done, such as a wood-destroying organism inspection or a prepaid hazard insurance policy.

PROGRESS QUIZ

44. The reason that a title searcher will look for public records in the buyer's name is to be certain
   a. the buyer is who the buyer claims to be.
   b. the buyer has no judgment liens that would "jump" on the title before the mortgage could be recorded.
   c. there are no judgments against the seller.
   d. all liens on the property have been paid or will be satisfied at closing.

Getting Documents before Closing

A common complaint of licensees is that documents are not available until just before the closing. This practice makes a careful review of the documents before closing difficult, if not impossible. The closing agent is the focus of the problem, but is usually unable to provide the statements because the lender has not completed the closing package. As in most problems of this nature, all parties working together may find a solution.

Proofreading the Closing Package

The final part of preclosing preparations is a complete review of the closing package. Items the closing agent must review on every document include the following:

- Names, dates, and legal descriptions
- Loan information
- Loan closing costs
- Calculations for recording fees, documentary stamp taxes, intangible taxes, discount points, origination fees, and brokers' commissions
- Survey exceptions
- Wood-destroying organism inspections
- Correct prorations of shared income and expenses

The closing agent must balance the HUD-1 statement with the total amount in checks to be disbursed. Receipts must equal disbursements.

IN PRACTICE

Check Out the Closing Statement

You should carefully check the closing statement. If you are working with the seller, compare the contract and the estimated seller's net proceeds statement prepared at the time of contract with the documents. The seller's proceeds as shown on the HUD-1 form should be at least as much as shown on the estimate, or you may have a problem. You should reconcile any differences. Often there is a larger-than-expected interest proration on the mortgage payoff.

If you are working with a buyer, start with the contract and the lender's good-faith estimate. If the HUD-1 form shows the buyer must have more cash than the good-faith estimate to close, you'll have to reconcile the difference.

IN PRACTICE

Get the Closing Documents to the Parties Before Closing

When you are finished proofreading the documents, make an appointment to deliver the documents to the buyer or seller. You should review the HUD-1 statement, compare it with the estimate, and discuss any differences. The buyer or seller will have an opportunity to look at all the available paperwork before the closing and raise any questions.

AT THE CLOSING TABLE

The closing would normally include the buyers, the sellers, and their respective licensees, if any. Sometimes attorneys of the parties attend and, occasionally, a lender's representative. The title closing agent conducts the closing.

Separate Closings

Many licensees prefer that buyers and sellers close separately rather than at the same closing table. This reduces confusion and allows the title closing agent to focus completely on each party as each closes. It is appropriate if the parties have had a dispute over some issue. Sometimes separate closings occur when there is a mail-away closing package or when the buyer or seller lives out of town.

Closing Disputes

The title closer is not an advocate for any of the parties. It is the title closer's job to close the transaction based on the contract and the lender's closing instructions. If there is a problem between the buyer and the lender, the closer gets them together on the phone. If there is a dispute between the buyer and the seller, the closer steps out of the room until the dispute is settled and the parties are ready to close.

Truth-in-Lending Disclosure

If there is an institutional loan, the first document to be reviewed must be the Truth-in-Lending (TIL) disclosure. If the buyers were informed by the lender or the licensee when they applied for the loan that the annual percentage rate (APR) shown on the TIL would be higher than the interest rate on their note, this will not be a problem. If they were not informed, however, some buyers, upon seeing a $7^1/_8$ percent APR on the disclosure form say, "Wait a minute! I was supposed to be getting a $7^1/_2$ percent loan!" The closer must explain that origination fees and discount points are included to calculate the APR, but the loan rate remains the same.

Loan Application

Usually the lender will want a typed loan application signed at closing, verifying the information given to the lender at the time of application.

Promissory Note

The note is the borrower's promise to pay. The closer presents the note for the buyer's signature. The note shows the principal balance, number of payments, and the dates and the amount of the payments. The amount will be for principal and interest only. The first payment date will normally be the first day of the second month after closing. The note is not witnessed or notarized. If a signature appears on the face of the note along with the borrower's signature, that person becomes a cosigner on the note.

PROGRESS QUIZ

45. When at the closing of her new home, a buyer claims to the sales associate, "Wait! You said my interest rate would be 7 percent. This paper shows the annual percentage rate is 7.42 percent." The sales associate probably failed to explain at the time she wrote the contract that
    a. the interest rate was subject to change between the time of loan application and closing.
    b. title companies often make mistakes in their calculations.
    c. the annual percentage rate will be higher than the note rate because of additional fees paid, such as discount points and origination fees.
    d. the federal government has weird ways of making the calculation for the annual percentage rate.

Mortgage

The mortgage is the security for the note. It is the document that may require the borrower to pay $^1/_{12}$ of the ad valorem taxes, hazard insurance, and mortgage insurance premium along with the principal and interest required by the note. It requires that payments be made on time, taxes be paid, and the property be covered by insurance. It also describes prepayment options and probably states that a transfer of the property will make the loan due immediately.

The General Warranty Deed

The deed is the document that transfers ownership of the real property. The general warranty deed is the most common deed, with the seller's guarantee to the buyer that the seller has good title, without material defects or encumbrances, and will stand by the guarantee forever. Special attention should be given to names, legal descriptions, and any items in the "subject to" section, such as restrictive covenants and mortgages.

Other Documents

Some of the other documents the buyer may sign include an anticoercion statement that the lender did not require the buyer to choose a certain insurance company. The lender and title insurance company will want a compliance agreement that the parties will do anything necessary to give the lender an acceptable loan package, such as signing new documents, if required. If the loan is above 80 percent of a home's value, the lender will want an affidavit that the buyer will occupy the property. The seller will be required to sign an affidavit that (1) the seller owns the property, (2) the seller has the right to convey it, and (3) the property is not encumbered by any lien or right to a lien, such as a construction lien.

Disbursements at Closing

Everyone expects to be paid at closing. This is not always possible, and licensees should be prepared to explain the problem to the sellers. Some title insurance companies agree to disburse the proceeds at closing if the certified checks will be deposited by the close of business that day. (A real estate broker may never do this.) Many title insurance companies will not disburse if the closing takes place too late to make a same-day deposit or if the lender is holding the loan proceeds check until the loan package is delivered.

Warehousing

Some companies hesitate to insure title until the "gap" between the time of the title commitment and the time of recording is checked. Any documents filed against the property during the gap period may affect the title. A lot depends on whether the title insurance company has any reason to suspect problems.

After the closing, all deposits are made by the title company, and the deeds and mortgages are copied for the lender's package before they are taken for recording. The closing package is prepared for the lender, awaiting only the recording information. When the documents are recorded, the information, including the date, time, and book and page numbers, is entered into the final title insurance policy and the package is sent to the lender.

When the recorded instruments are returned, the closing agent sends the buyer the original deed with recording information, a copy of the mortgage (the lender gets the original), and the title insurance policy.

Case Study

BROKER INADVERTENTLY OPERATES WITHOUT A CURRENT, ACTIVE LICENSE

● **Facts:** Respondents in this case are a for-profit corporation holding itself out to be a Florida brokerage company, the owner of the company, and the broker of the company.

1. In August 2004, the owner and the broker formed a real estate corporation. The broker registered the corporation with the local Board of Realtors and assumed that was adequate to operate the company as a real estate brokerage firm, but never registered the corporation with the DBPR.

2. In April 2008, the broker prepared a contract for sale showing the corporation as the listing broker. When the sale closed, one half of the commission was paid by the broker to another real estate firm that was in fact the listing broker. The other firm was not even aware of the sale until it received the commission check.

3. After a complaint was filed against the broker, the DBPR investigator discovered that the company was not licensed as a brokerage firm, and that the broker was not licensed because she had failed to complete all 14 hours of her continuing education for her last renewal. The broker immediately took care of the education and renewed her license. She had mistakenly assumed that the corporation was properly registered because she paid dues for it to the local Board of Realtors.

● **Questions:**

1. Which of the Respondents has committed a violation of Chapter 475?

_____

_____

_____

2. What penalties should be assessed against the guilty respondents?

_____

_____

_____

● **Determination of Violation:** The administrative law judge (ALJ) found that all parties were in violation of Chapter 475.42.(a): "...A person may not operate as a broker or sales associate without being the holder of a valid and current active license therefor..." The ALJ determined that the broker had no intent to defraud anyone or to do anything illegal or improper, but had nonetheless violated the law, and recommended that the brokerage firm and the owner be fined $5,000 each, and that the broker be fined $250 and suspended for one year.

● **Penalty:** The Florida Real Estate Commission entered a final order fining the brokerage firm and the owner $5,000 each. The broker was fined $250 and her license was suspended for one year.

Progress Test Answer Key

Note to the student:
If you have any questions about this course, the progress test, or the final examination, please contact the school or college where you obtained this material. Page numbers refer the reader to answers.

Item	Answer	Page	Item	Answer	Page
Chapter 1			**Chapter 3**		
1.	c	(2)	14.	d	(42)
2.	a	(3)	15.	d	(46)
3.	b	(5)	16.	c	(47)
4.	d	(6)	17.	c	(53)
5.	c	(7)	18.	d	(54)
6.	c	(9)			
7.	b	(10)	**Chapter 4**		
8.	c	(10)	19.	b	(64)
9.	b	(12)	20.	c	(65)
			21.	b	(66)
Chapter 2			22.	d	(69)
10.	c	(18)	23.	d	(68)
11.	b	(20)	24.	d	(71)
12.	a	(21)	25.	d	(71)
13.	a	(26)			

Item	Answer	Page	Item	Answer	Page
Chapter 5			**Chapter 7**		
26.	c	(76)	36.	b	(109)
27.	d	(76)	37.	b	(110)
28.	a	(78)	38.	d	(112)
29.	c	(82)	39.	b	(112)
30.	d	(86)			
			Chapter 8		
Chapter 6			40.	c	(120)
31.	a	(89)	41.	c	(120)
32.	b	(90)	42.	b	(123)
33.	d	(95)	43.	a	(128)
34.	d	(94)	44.	b	(128)
35.	c	(96)	45.	c	(131)

REQUEST FOR FEEDBACK ON COURSE

We welcome and encourage your feedback on *Continuing Education for Florida Real Estate Professionals,* 11th Edition. Your comments and suggestions about the course content will be used to evaluate this edition and plan changes for future editions.

Please be sure to indicate that you used the eleventh edition of *Continuing Education for Florida Real Estate Professionals* and send your comments to Dearborn Real Estate Education, Attention: Editorial Department, 332 Front Street South, Suite 501, La Crosse, WI 54601, or contact us through our Web site, *www.dearbornre.com.*

Forms-To-Go

TO OUR STUDENTS:

This forms resource is designed for real estate professionals. These forms have been carefully prepared and may be freely copied and used. While we believe the forms to be complete and accurate, we make no representation as to their legality. Before using these forms, licensees are cautioned to seek legal and professional advice.

Forms Included in This Section

*The Buyer disclosure forms are from the Tallahassee Board of REALTORS® and are used with permission.

Request for Address or Name Change

DBPR 0080-1 – Request for Address or Name Change

STATE OF FLORIDA
DEPARTMENT OF BUSINESS AND
PROFESSIONAL REGULATION

SELECT TRANSACTION TYPE

Transaction Type:
- ☐ Name Change (individual)
- ☐ Name Change (business)
- ☐ Change Mailing Address
- ☐ Change Contact Information (phone and/or e-mail)
- ☐ Change Physical Address

LICENSEE INFORMATION

License Number

Licensee Name (previous)

Licensee Name (new)

NEW MAILING ADDRESS

Street Address or P.O. Box

City	State	Zip Code (+4 optional)

County (if Florida address)	Country

NEW CONTACT INFORMATION

Primary Phone Number	Primary E-Mail Address

NEW PHYSICAL ADDRESS (IF DIFFERENT THAN MAILING ADDRESS)

Street Address

City	State	Zip Code (+4 optional)

County (if Florida address)	Country

NEW ADDITIONAL CONTACT INFORMATION (OPTIONAL)

Alternate Phone Number	Fax Number

Alternate E-Mail Address

I affirm that I have provided the above information completely and truthfully to the best of my knowledge.

Licensee Sign Here:_____ Date: _____

Request for Change of Status

DBPR RE-2050 – Request for Change of Status

STATE OF FLORIDA
DEPARTMENT OF BUSINESS AND PROFESSIONAL REGULATION
1940 North Monroe Street
Tallahassee, FL 32399-0783
Customer Contact Center: 850.487.1395
FAX: 850.488.8040
www.myfloridalicense.com/dbpr

CHECK ACTION(S) REQUESTED

Transaction Type:
- ❏ Become Active – no charge
- ❏ Become Inactive – no charge
- ❏ Add/Delete Trade Name – no charge
- ❏ Become Sole Proprietor – no charge (Forms 2050 & 0080 required)
- ❏ Change Broker/Owner Employer – no charge
- ❏ Terminate Employee – no charge
- ❏ Add/Delete PA or LLC - $30.00 fee required – see F.S. 475.161
- ❏ Request for Multiple License - $95.00
- ❏ Renew license
- ❏ Qualifying Broker (CQ package required)
- ❏ Owner/Developer (Forms 2050 & 0080 required)

ASSOCIATE INFORMATION

License Number	Licensee Name

Contact Information (telephone number or E-Mail address)

BROKER OR ORGANIZATION INFORMATION

Broker License Number	Organization License Number

Broker/Owner Name

Organization Name

Trade Name (if applicable)	Contact Info. (telephone number or E-Mail address)

Are you now or with the issuance of this license, an officer, director, member, or partner of any corporation, partnership, or L.L.C. which acts as a broker? Yes ❏ No ❏
If yes, please list name of entity

ATTEST STATEMENT
REQUIRES SIGNATURE OF BROKER <u>AND</u> ASSOCIATE*
(Except for Add/Delete PA or LLC – which may be signed by the licensee)

I affirm that I have provided the above information completely and truthfully to the best of my knowledge.

Broker/Owner Sign Here: _____ Date: _____
*Broker signature not req. for Assoc. inactive status or add/delete PA –LLC

Print Broker/Owner Name: _____

Associate Sign Here: _____ Date: _____
*All Associate requested changes require signature

Charlie Crist, Governor
Holly Benson, Secretary

Department of Business
Professional Regulation &

Division of Real Estate
Thomas O'Bryant, Director
400 West Robinson Street, N801
Orlando, Florida 32801-1757

Phone: 407.481.5662
Fax: 407.317.7245
www.MyFlorida.com/dbpr
www.MyFloridaLicense.com

NOTICE OF ESCROW DISPUTE/GOOD FAITH DOUBT
(Please Type or Print CLEARLY)

I. Broker Information

Name of broker _____ Broker license no. _____

Street address_____Telephone_____

City_____ State_____ Zip_____

E-mail address _____ Brokerage firm_____

In compliance with Section 475.25(1)(d)1., Florida Statutes, Rule 61J2-10.032, Florida

Administrative Code, be advised that broker has (**check one**):

_____received conflicting demands

_____good faith doubt as to which party is entitled to the deposit in broker's escrow account in

the amount of $_____

Date _____

II. Parties to the transaction

___Seller ___Landlord

Name _____

Street address or Box no. _____

City_____ State_____ Zip_____

___Buyer ___Tenant

Name _____

Street address or Box no. _____

City_____ State_____ Zip_____

III. Property

This notice concerns the property located at:

Street address _____

City _____ State_____ Zip _____

DEPARTMENT OF BUSINESS & PROFESSIONAL REGULATION
DIVISION OF REAL ESTATE

Charlie Crist, *Governor*   Holly Benson, *Secretary*

REQUEST FOR ESCROW DISBURSEMENT ORDER
(Please type or print CLEARLY)

I. PROFILE INFORMATION

Name of requesting broker_____

Street address_____

City_____ State_____ Zip_____

Name of requesting brokerage_____

CHECK ONE OR BOTH

☐ Listing Office   ☐ Selling Office

Telephone_____

E-mail_____

Broker license no._____

Name of co-broker (if any) _____

Name of brokerage_____

Street address _____

City_____ State_____ Zip_____

CHECK ONE

☐ Listing Office   ☐ Selling Office

Telephone_____

E-mail_____

Broker license no._____

Name of purchaser/lessee_____

Current* street address _____

City_____ State_____ Zip_____

Name of attorney (if any)_____

Telephone:_____

Other:_____

*Please keep us advised of any address changes.

Name of seller/lessor_____

Current* street address _____

City_____ State_____ Zip_____

Name of attorney (if any)_____

Telephone:_____

Other:_____

*Please keep us advised of any address changes.

Directions to Broker:

1. The broker holding the escrow deposit must complete this form FULLY by answering each question and attaching LEGIBLE copies of all supporting documents and correspondence. DBPR will return incomplete or undocumented requests.

2. Return the completed form to the Department of Business and Professional Regulation, Division of Real Estate, 400 West Robinson Street, Suite N802, Orlando, Florida 32801.

3. THE REQUESTING BROKER MUST SIGN AND DATE ON PAGE THREE OF THIS FORM.

4. If the parties later elect to arbitrate, mediate, interplead or litigate this matter or if the parties arrive at a resolution after the date of this request, the requesting broker must notify DRE within 10 business days.

5. Use additional sheets if necessary.

Request for Escrow Disbursement Order (continued)

Request for Escrow Disbursement Order

II. Funds and Financing

A. Amount of funds held by broker $_____

B. Total purchase price/lease price $_____

C. Funds are held in: ☐ Listing office trust account   ☐ Selling office trust account   ☐ Other (please explain in detail below)

D. Have purchaser/lessee and seller/lessee executed a sales contract or other agreement?

☐ Yes   ☐ No   ☐ Other (Please explain in detail below)

If Yes, attach a complete, legible copy of the executed contract or agreement with addenda/riders.

Effective date of contract or agreement: _____

Date(s) Deposit(s) made to broker's trust account: _____

E. If mortgage financing is involved, did purchaser make application for financing?   ☐ Yes   ☐ No

If Yes, provide the information requested below:

Applications was: ☐ Approved   ☐ Denied

Date:

Reasons for denial and subsequent financial history:
(attach lender's statement of denial if available)

Request for Escrow Disbursement Order (continued)

Request for Escrow Disbursement Order

III. Area of Dispute

A. Has purchaser/lessee requested (of you or of co-broker) the return of the deposit? ☐ Yes   ☐ No

If Yes, please give date and purchaser's/lessee's reason for requesting such refund (attach copies of relevant correspondence):

Date:

Reason:

B. Has seller/lessor made demand (of you or of co-broker) for forfeiture of the deposit? ☐ Yes   ☐ No

If Yes, please give date and seller's/lessor's reason for claiming a forfeiture (attach copies of relevant correspondence):

Date:

Reason:

C. Please list the names, addresses and telephone numbers of anyone who may have additional information relative to this matter. Include any comments you feel may assist The Florida Real Estate Commission in the determination of this matter.

IV. Certification

Under penalties of perjury, I declare that I have read the foregoing and the facts alleged are true, to the best of my knowledge and belief. All exhibits attached are true copies of the originals made by me or under my supervision. I understand that my representations have been made for the express purpose of securing an escrow disbursement order from the Florida Real Estate Commission. I further understand that any false statements shall subject me to the provisions of Section 475.25, Florida Statutes, and may be punishable under the provisions of Section 837.06, Florida Statutes.

_____   _____

Date   Signature of requesting broker

NO BROKERAGE RELATIONSHIP NOTICE

FLORIDA LAW REQUIRES THAT THE REAL ESTATE LICENSEES WHO HAVE NO BROKERAGE RELATIONSHIP WITH A POTENTIAL SELLER OR BUYER DISCLOSE THEIR DUTIES TO SELLERS AND BUYERS.

As a real estate licensee who has no brokerage relationship with you, _____ *(insert name of Real Estate Entity)* and its Associates owe to you the following duties:

1. Dealing honestly and fairly.
2. Disclosing all known facts that materially affect the value of residential real property which are not readily observable to the buyer.
3. Accounting for all funds entrusted to the licensee.

_____   _____
Date   Signature

_____   _____
Date   Signature

SINGLE AGENT NOTICE

FLORIDA LAW REQUIRES THAT THE REAL ESTATE LICENSEES OPERATING AS SINGLE AGENTS DISCLOSE TO THE BUYERS AND SELLERS THEIR DUTIES.

As a single agent _____ *(insert name of Real Estate Entity and its Associates)* owe to you the following duties:

1. Dealing honestly and fairly;

2. Loyalty;

3. Confidentiality;

4. Obedience;

5. Full disclosure;

6. Accounting for all funds;

7. Skill, care, and diligence in the transaction;

8. Presenting all offers and counteroffers in a timely manner, unless a party has previously directed the licensee otherwise in writing; and

9. Disclosing all known facts that materially affect the value of residential real property and are not readily observable.

_____   _____
Signature   Date

_____   _____
Signature   Date

CONSENT TO TRANSITION TO TRANSACTION BROKER

FLORIDA LAW ALLOWS REAL ESTATE LICENSEES WHO REPRESENT A BUYER OR SELLER AS A SINGLE AGENT TO CHANGE FROM A SINGLE AGENT RELATIONSHIP TO A TRANSACTION BROKERAGE RELATIONSHIP IN ORDER FOR THE LICENSEE TO ASSIST BOTH PARTIES IN A REAL ESTATE TRANSACTION BY PROVIDING A LIMITED FORM OF REPRESENTATION TO BOTH THE BUYER AND THE SELLER. THIS CHANGE IN RELATIONSHIP CANNOT OCCUR WITHOUT YOUR PRIOR WRITTEN CONSENT.

As a transaction broker _____ provides to
(insert name of Real Estate Firm and its Associates)
you a limited form of represensentation that includes the following duties:

1. Dealing honestly and fairly;

2. Accounting for all funds;

3. Using skill, care, and diligence in the transaction;

4. Disclosing all known facts that materially affect the value of residential real property and are not readily observable;

5. Presenting all offers and counteroffers in a timely manner, unless a party has previously directed the licensee otherwise in writing;

6. Limited confidentiality, unless waived in writing by a party. This limited confidentiality will prevent disclosure that the seller will accept a price less than the asking or listed price, that the buyer will pay a price greater than the price submitted in a written offer, of the motivation of any party for selling or buying property, that a seller or buyer will agree to financing terms other than those offered, or of any other information requested by a party to remain confidential; and

7. Any additional duties that are entered into by this or by separate written agreement.

Limited representation means that a buyer or seller is not responsible for the acts of the licensee. Additionally, parties are giving up their rights to the undivided loyalty of the licensee. This aspect of limited representation allows a licensee to facilitate a real estate transaction by assisting both the buyer and the seller, but a licensee will not work to represent one party to the detriment of the other party when acting as a transaction broker to both parties.

I agree that my agent may assume the role and duties of a transaction broker.

[Must be initialed or signed]

_____   _____
Signature   Date

_____   _____
Signature   Date

Designated Sales Associate Notice

DESIGNATED SALES ASSOCIATE

I have assets of one million dollars or more. I request that _____

(Name of broker)

use the designated sales associate form of representation.

SINGLE AGENT NOTICE

FLORIDA LAW REQUIRES THAT THE REAL ESTATE LICENSEES OPERATING AS SINGLE AGENTS DISCLOSE TO THE BUYERS AND SELLERS THEIR DUTIES.

As a single agent _____ owe to you the

(insert name of Real Estate Entity and its Associates)

following duties:

1. Dealing honestly and fairly;

2. Loyalty;

3. Confidentiality;

4. Obedience;

5. Full disclosure;

6. Accounting for all funds;

7. Skill, care, and diligence in the transaction;

8. Presenting all offers and counteroffers in a timely manner, unless a party has previously directed the licensee otherwise in writing; and

9. Disclosing all known facts that materially affect the value of residential real property and are not readily observable.

_____   _____

Signature   Date

DESIGNATED SALES ASSOCIATE NOTICE

Florida law prohibits a designated sales associate from disclosing, except to the broker or persons specified by the broker, information made confidential by request or at the instruction of the customer the designated sales associate is representing. However, Florida law allows a designated sales associate to disclose information allowed to be disclosed or required to be disclosed by law and also allows a designated sales associate to disclose to his or her broker, or persons specified by the broker, confidential information of a customer for the purpose of seeking advice or assistance for the benefit of the customer in regard to a transaction. Florida law requires that the broker must hold this information confidential and may not use such information to the detriment of the other party.

_____   _____   _____

Date   Signature optional   Signature optional

Disclosure of Lead-Based Paint and Lead-Based Paint Hazards

LEAD-BASED PAINT OR LEAD-BASED PAINT HAZARD ADDENDUM

It is a condition of this contract that, until midnight of _____ , Buyer shall have the right to obtain a risk assessment or inspection of the Property for the presence of lead-based paint and/or lead-based paint hazards* at Buyer's expense. This contingency will terminate at that time unless Buyer or Buyer's agent delivers to the Seller or Seller's agent a written inspection and/or risk assessment report listing the specific existing deficiencies and corrections needed, if any. If any corrections are necessary, Seller shall have the option of (i) completing them, (ii) providing for their completion, or (iii) refusing to complete them. If Seller elects not to complete or provide for completion of the corrections, then Buyer shall have the option of (iv) accepting the Property in its present condition, or (v) terminating this contract, in which case all earnest monies shall be refunded to Buyer. Buyer may waive the right to obtain a risk assessment or inspection of the Property for the presence of lead-based paint and/or lead based paint hazards at any time without cause.

*Intact lead-based paint that is in good condition is not necessarily a hazard. See EPA pamphlet *Protect Your Family From Lead in Your Home* for more information.

Disclosure of Information on Lead-Based Paint and Lead-Based Paint Hazards

Lead Warning Statement

Every Buyer of any interest in residential real property on which a residential dwelling was built prior to 1978 is notified that such property may present exposure to lead from lead-based paint that may place young children at risk of developing lead poisoning. Lead poisoning in young children may produce permanent neurological damage, including learning disabilities, reduced intelligence quotient, behavioral problems, and impaired memory. Lead poisoning also poses a particular risk to pregnant women. The Seller of any interest in residential real property is required to provide the Buyer with any information on lead-based paint hazards from risk assessments or inspections in the Seller's possession and notify the Buyer of any known lead-based paint hazards. A risk assessment or inspection for possible lead-based paint hazards is recommended prior to purchase.

Seller's Disclosure (initial)

_____ (a) Presence of lead-based paint and/or lead-based paint hazards (check one below):

❑ Known lead-based paint and/or lead-based paint hazards are present in the housing (explain).

_____
_____

❑ Seller has no knowledge of lead-based paint and/or lead-based paint hazards in the housing.

_____ (b) Records and reports available to the Seller (check one below):

❑ Seller has provided the Buyer with all available records and reports pertaining to lead-based paint and/or lead-based paint hazards in the housing (list documents below).

_____
_____

❑ Seller has no reports or records pertaining to lead-based paint and/or lead-based paint hazards in the housing.

Buyer's Acknowledgment (initial)

_____ (c) Buyer has received copies of all information listed above.

_____ (d) Buyer has received the pamphlet *Protect Your Family from Lead in Your Home.*

_____ (e) Buyer has (check one below):

❑ Received a 10-day opportunity (or mutually agreed upon period) to conduct a risk assessment or inspection for the presence of lead-based paint and/or lead-based paint hazards; or

❑ Waived the opportunity to conduct a risk assessment or inspection for the presence of lead-based paint and/or lead-based paint hazards.

Agent's Acknowledgment (initial)

_____ (f) Agent has informed the Seller of the Seller's obligations under 42 U.S.C. 4582(d) and is aware of his/her responsibility to ensure compliance.

Certification of Accuracy

The following parties have reviewed the information above and certify, to the best of their knowledge, that the information provided by the signatory is true and accurate.

Buyer: _____ (SEAL) Date _____
Buyer: _____ (SEAL) Date _____
Agent: _____ Date _____
Seller: _____ (SEAL) Date _____
Seller: _____ (SEAL) Date _____
Agent: _____ Date _____

Fair Housing Poster

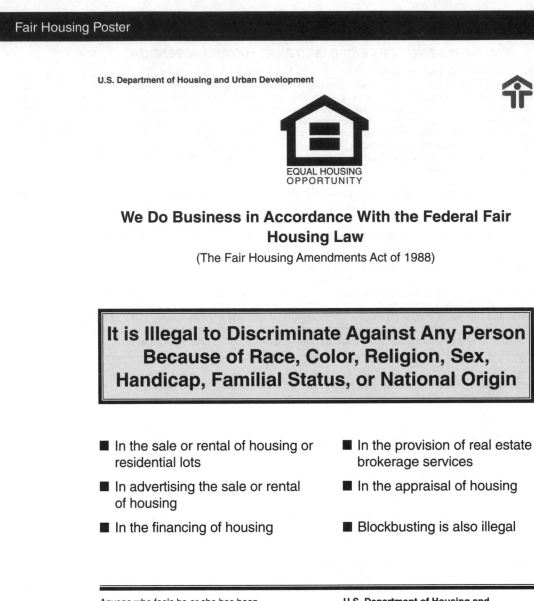

U.S. Department of Housing and Urban Development

EQUAL HOUSING
OPPORTUNITY

We Do Business in Accordance With the Federal Fair Housing Law

(The Fair Housing Amendments Act of 1988)

It is Illegal to Discriminate Against Any Person Because of Race, Color, Religion, Sex, Handicap, Familial Status, or National Origin

- ■ In the sale or rental of housing or residential lots
- ■ In advertising the sale or rental of housing
- ■ In the financing of housing

- ■ In the provision of real estate brokerage services
- ■ In the appraisal of housing
- ■ Blockbusting is also illegal

Anyone who feels he or she has been discriminated against may file a complaint of housing discrimination:
  1-800-669-9777 (Toll Free)
  1-800-927-9275 (TDD)

**U.S. Department of Housing and Urban Development
Assistant Secretary for Fair Housing and Equal Opportunity
Washington, D.C. 20410**

Previous editions are obsolete

form HUD-928.1A (2/2003)

Escrow Account Reconciliation Form (Monthly Reconciliation Statement)

REAL ESTATE ESCROW ACCOUNT
Monthly Reconciliation Statement

Reconciliation for Month of: _____

Date Reconciliation Performed: _____

Bank Statement Period: _____

Account Name: _____

Name of Bank: _____

Account Number: _____

I. BANK RECONCILIATION

(1) Balance per Bank Statement: $_____

Outstanding Checks

Date	Check #	Amount	Date	Check #	Amount

(2) Total of Outstanding Checks: $_____

(3) Balance after Deducting Outstanding Checks: $_____

Date	Check #	Amount	Date	Check #	Amount

(4) Plus Total Amount of Deposits in Transit: $_____

(5) Reconciled Bank Balance: $_____

YOU ARE NOT FINISHED.

The Reconciled Bank Balance must be compared to Broker's Trust Liability. Complete next page.

Escrow Account Reconciliation Form (Monthly Reconciliation Statement) (continued)

II. BROKER'S TRUST LIABILITY RECONCILIATION:

Itemized list of broker's trust liability:

Customer Name	Amount	Customer Name	Amount

(6) Total of Broker's Trust Liability $_____

(7) Adjusted Bank Balance: (*from line 5, previous page*) $_____

Check one of the following:

❏ (A) Adjusted Bank Balance (Line 7) and Broker's Trust Liability (Line 6) <u>DO</u> agree.

❏ (B) Adjusted Bank Balance (Line 7) and Broker's Trust Liability (Line 6) <u>DO NOT</u> agree.

If you checked (B), you must complete the following to explain the difference between adjusted bank balance (Line 4) and Broker's Trust Liabillity (Line 5):

SHORTAGE: (If Line 7 is less than Line 6)   Total Shortage: $_____

Reason for Shortage (i.e., NSF, service charge, negative balance): _____
_____

Corrective Action Taken: _____

<u>OVERAGE:</u> (If Line 4 is more than Line 5)   Total Overage:
$ _____ $ _____

Reason for overage (i.e., Broker's funds up to $200 in account, etc.): _____
_____

Corrective Action Taken: _____

I, _____, Broker, have reviewed this monthly
      reconciliation.

Broker's Signature: _____

Date: _____

COMPREHENSIVE BUYER'S DISCLOSURES

PROPERTY
ADDRESS:_____

1) RADON GAS: Radon is a naturally occurring radioactive gas that, when it has accumulated in a building in sufficient quantities, may present health risks to persons who are exposed to it over a period of time. Levels of radon that exceed federal and state guidelines have been found in buildings in Florida. Additional information regarding radon and radon testing may be obtained from your county public health unit. (Section 404.056(8), F.S.)

2) BUILDING ENERGY EFFICIENCY: BUYER may have the energy efficiency of the building they are purchasing determined pursuant to Florida Statute 553.996. BUYER acknowledges receipt of the Florida Building Energy-Efficiency Rating System Information Brochure.

3) PROPERTY TAXES: BUYER should not rely on the SELLER'S current property taxes as the amount of property taxes that the BUYER may be obligated to pay in the year subsequent to purchase. A change of ownership or property improvements triggers reassessments of the property that could result in higher property taxes. If you have questions concerning valuation, contact the county property appraiser's office for information.

4) SQUARE FOOTAGE: BUYER acknowledges they have not relied upon BROKER'S or SELLER'S estimate of square footage of property. Square footage is approximate and may have been provided by third party sources. If square footage is of concern to BUYER, the BUYER is advised to personally measure the property.

5) SCHOOL ZONES: BUYER is advised to verify schools zones and possible school and grade level caps through the local school board.

6) INSPECTIONS: BUYER is strongly advised to obtain property and whole house inspection(s) as provided for in the Contract for Sale and Purchase. BUYER should select professionals with appropriate qualifications to conduct inspections. BUYER is advised that some properties may have materials (such as, but not limited to, Louisiana Pacific and Synthetic Stucco) that have failed the manufacturer's warranties and/or have been known to have defects, and that inspection is one way to identify this and determine the condition of these materials. BUYER is aware that BROKERS and their SALES ASSOCIATES do not guarantee nor warrant the condition of the property and are in no way responsible for the condition of the property.

7) LAND USE DISCLAIMER: Due to the unpredictable and constantly changing status of the municipal, county and state regulations for property development, the SELLER and the SALES ASSOCIATE(S) and/or BROKER(S) involved in this transaction have found it necessary to clarify their duties and obligations with regard to the sale or lease of the property. The BUYER recognizes that the City and/or County where the property is located has a Comprehensive Land Use Plan. It is the BUYER'S obligation to contact the appropriate local government department(s) to determine how the subject property may be affected by the Comprehensive Plan and take any necessary action to ensure compliance with the plan. Additionally, the subject property may be affected by restrictive covenants, zoning, and/or other land use restrictions. If so, it shall be the BUYER'S' responsibility to inquire about them in no less a degree than as hereinafter provided.

BUYER is hereby advised that it is the BUYER'S responsibility to determine whether or not the subject property lies within the City or only the County. Both may have separate zoning and/or land use regulations, which would affect the subject property. It shall also be the BUYER'S sole responsibility to inquire into any state and local governmental zoning and land use regulations and restrictive covenants to determine whether the subject property is in compliance with all state and local government laws, codes and ordinances, and restrictive covenants. The BUYER understands that the SELLER and the SALES

Sample Comprehensive Buyer's Disclosures (continued)

ASSOCIATE(S) and/or BROKER(S) make no representations as to whether the subject property is suitable for any particular use and that the BUYER shall be solely obligated to make any and all necessary inquiries with the appropriate governing bodies to determine compliance with all applicable zoning, land use regulations, and restrictive covenants. The BUYER further releases the SELLER and the SALES ASSOCIATE(S) and/or BROKER(S) for any statements or comments made in relation to the potential use of the subject property.

8) ROAD AND DRAINAGE FACILITY MAINTENANCE DISCLOSURE: The BUYER may be responsible for the maintenance of roads and related drainage, if any, serving this Property, and unless there is an ownership interest in such roads and related drainage by governmental authorities, said governmental authority shall have no responsibility for such maintenance.

9) RESTRICTIVE COVENANTS: Applicable Homeowner's Association should be contacted for any questions concerning property use and/or restrictions and assessments. It is the responsibility of the BUYER to ascertain the restrictive covenants and homeowner association documents are complete and the most current. BUYER has been advised to read the Restrictive Covenants related to the subject property. BUYER acknowledges prior to contract:
☐ BUYER has been provided with a copy of the restrictive covenants related to the subject property.
☐ This contract is contingent upon ☐☐ BUYER ☐☐ SELLER providing to BUYER within 5 days of acceptance of this contract by all parties Restrictive Covenants. BUYER has 2 days after receipt to review and find them acceptable.

10) SELLER'S PROPERTY DISCLOSURE; HOMEOWNERS' ASSOCIATION/COMMUNITY DISCLOSURE:
☐ BUYER has been provided with a copy of the Seller's Property Disclosure containing the Homeowner's Association/Community Disclosure prior to contract.
☐ This contract is contingent upon SELLER executing and providing to BUYER, within 5 days of acceptance of this contract by all parties, the Tallahassee Board of Realtors Seller's Property Disclosure containing the Homeowner's Association/Community Disclosure. The BUYER has 2 days after receipt to review and find it acceptable.

11) BUILDER'S WARRANTY (NEW CONSTRUCTION ONLY):
☐ BUYER has been provided a copy of the SELLER's written warranty and accepts it.
☐ BUYER has been advised there is no written warranty.
☐ This contract is contingent upon SELLER providing to BUYER, within 5 days of acceptance of this contract by all parties, any written warranty provided by the SELLER. The BUYER has 2 days after receipt to review and find it acceptable.

If you do not understand some point, please ask us to explain it and do not sign any document until you clearly understand it. If you are not satisfied with any explanation provided, you are encouraged to consult a real estate attorney.

BY SIGNATURE BELOW, BUYER IS ACKNOWLEDGING THAT BUYER HAS READ AND UNDERSTANDS THE ABOVE DISCLOSURES PRIOR TO EXECUTION OF THE CONTRACT FOR SALE AND PURCHASE.

_____   _____
BUYER   DATE   Seller
DATE

_____   _____
BUYER   DATE   Seller
DATE

Homeowners' Association/Community Disclosure

HOMEOWNERS' ASSOCIATION/COMMUNITY DISCLOSURE

IF THE DISCLOSURE SUMMARY REQUIRED BY SECTION 689.26, F. S., HAS NOT BEEN PROVIDED TO THE PROSPECTIVE PURCHASER BEFORE EXECUTING THIS CONTRACT FOR SALE, THIS CONTRACT IS VOIDABLE BY BUYER BY DELIVERING TO SELLER OR SELLER'S AGENT WRITTEN NOTICE OF THE BUYER'S INTENTION TO CANCEL WITHIN 3 DAYS AFTER RECEIPT OF THE DISCLOSURE SUMMARY OR PRIOR TO CLOSING, WHICHEVER OCCURS FIRST. ANY PURPORTED WAIVER OF THIS VOIDABILITY RIGHT HAS NO EFFECT. BUYER'S RIGHT TO VOID THIS CONTRACT SHALL TERMINATE AT CLOSING.

Disclosure summary

For _____

(name of community)

1. As a purchaser of property in this community, you will be obligated to be a member of a homeowners' association.

2. There have been or will be recorded restrictive covenants governing the use and occupancy of properties in this community.

3. You will be obligated to pay assessments to the association. Assessments may be subject to periodic change. If applicable, the current amount is $_____ per _____. You will also be obligated to pay any special assessments imposed by the association. Such special assessments may be subject to change. If applicable, the current amount is $_____ per _____.

4. You may be obligated to pay special assessments to the respective municipality, county, or special district. All assessments are subject to periodic change.

5. Your failure to pay special assessments or assessments levied by a mandatory homeowners' association could result in a lien on your property.

6. There may be an obligation to pay rent or land use fees for recreational or other commonly used facilities as an obligation of membership in the homeowners' association. If applicable, the current amount is $_____ per _____.

7. The developer may have the right to amend the restrictive covenants without the approval of the association membership or the approval of the parcel owners.

8. The statements contained in this disclosure form are only summary in nature, and, as a prospective purchaser, you should refer to the covenants and the association governing documents before purchasing property.

9. These documents are either matters of public record and can be obtained from the record office in the county where the property is located, or are not recorded and can be obtained from the developer.

_____

Date

_____

Purchaser

_____

Purchaser

Property Sale Information Sheet

Property Address: _____

Seller: _____ Buyer: _____

Contract Date: _____ Closing Date (Est.): _____

Seller	Buyer

Listing Broker: _____

Phone: _____ Fax: _____
Listing sales associate: _____
Home Ph.: ____ Office Ph.: ____
Mobile Ph.: _____

Selling Broker: _____

Phone: _____ Fax: _____
Selling sales associate: _____
Home Ph.: ____ Office Ph.: ____
Mobile Ph.: _____

Seller: _____

Old address: _____
New address: _____
City, State, Zip _____
Current Home Ph.: ____ Ofc.: ____

Buyer: _____

Present address: _____
City, State, Zip _____
Current Home Ph.: ____ Ofc.: ____
Will buyer occupy new home? ____

Existing mortgage for Payoff (P)
Assumption (A)
1st Mortgage holder: _____
2nd Mortgage holder: _____

New Mortgage Lender: _____
Type (Fixed; ARM: FHA, VA, Conv.): ____
LTV Ratio: ___% Interest Rate: ___%
Yrs: ___

Seller's Attorney: _____
Ph.: _____

Buyer's Attorney: _____
Ph.: _____

Lender: _____ **Loan Officer:** _____

Title Company: _____ **Closing Agent:** _____

Appraiser: _____

Date Scheduled to Close: _____

Service Providers:

Pest inspection: _____ Ph.: _____
Home inspection: _____ Ph.: _____
Roof inspection: _____ Ph.: _____
Contractor: _____ Ph.: _____
Surveyor: _____ Ph.: _____

Buyer's Insurance Company: _____

Agent: _____ Phone: _____

Property status: ❏ Occupied by seller ❏ Occupied by tenant ❏ Vacant

Key to property for inspection: ❏ At listing office ❏ In lockbox at property ❏ Call seller for appointment

Closing Progress Chart

Property Address: _____

Seller: _____   Buyer: _____

Listing Sales Associate				Closing Progress Chart		Selling Sales Associate		
#	Sched Date	Actual Date	X	**Closing Duties**	Done √	X	Sched Date	Actual Date
1				"Sale pending" sign on listing				
2				Notice of under contract to MLS				
3				Binder deposited in bank $_____				
4				Additional binder received, if required $_____				
5				Loan application made by buyer				
6				Contingencies cleared in writing:				
7				Home inspection By: _____				
8				Soil test from: _____				
9				Roof inspection By: _____				
10				Other (describe): _____				
11				Appraisal By: _____				
12				Loan approval From: _____				
13				Title insurance ordered from: _____				
14				Pest inspection ordered (after loan approval) from:				
15				Report received and delivered to buyer				
16				Report received and delivered to lender				
17				Treatment ordered, if required				
18				Structure inspection ordered, if necessary				
19				Work completed and approved				
20				Required repairs ordered				
21				Required repairs completed				
22				Survey ordered (After loan approval)				
23				Survey completed. Results. . .				
24				Encroachments, survey problems cleared				
25				Buyer to get hazard insurance				
26				Insurance policy to title closing agent				
27				Buyer/seller contacted for closing appointment				
28				Pre-closing inspection				
29				Closing papers reviewed with buyer/seller 1 day prior				
30				Buyer given figure for certified check for closing				
31				Binder check prepared to take to closing				
32				Closing date				
33				Signed closing papers received by sales associate				
34				**Post-closing duties:**				
35				Commission check to broker				
36				Sign/lockbox picked up from property				
37				Buyer/seller letter of thanks				
38				Follow-up visit to buyer/seller				
39				Notice of closed sale to MLS				

NOTICE OF INTENTION TO
IMPOSE CLAIM ON SECURITY DEPOSIT

> Sent by Certified Mail,
> return receipt requested
> _____, 200___

A landlord must return a tenant's security deposit to the tenant no more than 15 days after the tenant leaves the leased property. The landlord may claim all or a portion of the security deposit only after giving the tenant written notice, by <u>certified mail</u> to the tenant's last known mailing address, of the landlord's intention to keep the deposit and the reason for keeping it. If the landlord does not send the notice within the 15 day period, the landlord cannot keep the security deposit. If the tenant does not object to the notice, the landlord may then keep the amount stated in the notice and must send the rest of the deposit to the tenant within 30 days after the date of the notice.

SOURCE: Section 83.49(3)(a), Florida Statutes

To: _____

Tenant's Name

_____

Address

_____

City/State/Zip

Date: _____

This is a notice of my intention to impose a claim for damages in the amount of

$_____ upon your security deposit due to: _____

_____.

It is sent to you as required by 83.49(3), Florida Statutes. You are hereby notified that

you must object in writing to this deduction from your security deposit within 15 days

from the time you receive this notice or I will be authorized to deduct my claim from your

security deposit. Your objection must be sent to:

_____

Landlord's Name

_____

Address

_____

Phone Number: _____

Notice of Dishonored Check

NOTICE OF DISHONORED CHECK

TO: _____

_____

_____

Sent by Certified Mail, return receipt requested _____, 200__

CRIMINAL PENALTIES

You are hereby notified that a check, numbered _____, in the face amount of $_____, issued by you on _____, 200 ____, drawn upon _____, and payble to _____, has been dishonored. Pursuant to Florida law, you have 7 days from receipt of this notice to tender payment of the full amount of such check plus a service charge of $25, if the face value does not exceed $50, $30, if the face value exceeds $50 but does not exceed $300, $40, if the face value exceeds $300, or an amount of up to 5 percent of the face amount of the check, whichever is greater, the total amount due being $_____ and _____ cents. Unless this amount is paid in full within the time specified above, the holder of such check may turn over the dishonored check and all other available information relating to this incident to the state attorney for criminal prosecution. You may be additionally liable in a civil action for triple the amount of the check, but in no case less than $50, together with the amount of the check, a service charge, court costs, reasonable attorney fees, and incurred bank fees, as provided in Chapter 68.065, Florida Statutes.

CIVIL REMEDIES

You are hereby notified that a check numbered _____ in the face amount of $_____, issued by you on _____, 200 _____, drawn upon _____, and payable to _____, has been dishonored. Pursuant to Florida law, you have 30 days from receipt of this notice to tender payment in cash of the full amount of the check plus a service charge of $25, if the face value does not exceed $50, $30, if the face value exceeds $50 but does not exceed $300, $40, if the face value exceeds $300, or 5 percent of the face amount of the check, whichever is greater, the total amount due being $_____ and _____ cents. Unless this amount is paid in full within the 30-day period, the holder of the check or instrument may file a civil action against you for three times the amount of the check, but in no case less than $50, in addition to the payment of the check plus any court costs, reasonable attorney fees, and any bank fees incurred by the payee in taking the action.

THREE-DAY NOTICE

To: _____

Tenant's Full Name

_____

Tenant's Address

_____

Tenant's City, State, ZIP

From: _____

Date: _____

You are hereby notified that you are indebted to me in the sum of $_____ for the rent and use of the premises located at:

_____

_____

_____,

Florida,

now occupied by you and that I demand payment of the rent or possession of the premises within three days (excluding Saturday, Sunday, and legal holidays) from the date of delivery of this notice, to wit: on or before the _____ day of _____, 20_____. (Insert the date which is three days from the delivery of this notice, excluding the date of delivery, Saturday, Sunday, and legal holidays.)

_____

Signature

_____

Name of Landlord/Property Manager

_____

Address

_____

City, State, ZIP Code

_____

Telephone Number

Index

Notes

Notes

Notes

Notes

Notes

Notes

Notes

Notes

Notes

Notes

Notes

Notes